ONE-DAY CRICKET

ONE-DAY CRICKET

Jim Laker

B.T. BATSFORD LTD · LONDON

First published 1977
© 1977 Jim Laker

ISBN 0 7134 0660 7
Typeset in Monophoto Plantin by
Servis Filmsetting Ltd, Manchester

Printed in Great Britain by
J.W. Arrowsmith Ltd, Bristol
for the Publishers,
B.T. Batsford Ltd,
4 Fitzhardinge Street,
London W1H 0AH

Contents

List of Illustrations

Acknowledgment

Copyright photographs in this book are reproduced by kind permission of Benson and Hedges Ltd, Gillette Industries, and Patrick Eagar.

Introduction

I am sure it will come as a surprise to many people to learn that the majority of cricket played in our islands now comes under the heading of 'limited overs'.

Even our County Championship cricket has unhappily been restricted to 100 overs per side for the first innings. For our first class cricketers there remains only Test Match cricket which to date has escaped any form of limitation, but is enjoyed only by a tiny and privileged percentage.

It seemed, therefore, that a book concentrated on the good, or possibly the evils, of the growth of instant cricket could well be a worthwhile exercise. It also quickly became apparent that it would be an impossible task to cover all the one-day cricket competitions both sponsored or otherwise which are played in the country. At the last count 23 were played Nationally and a further 127 contested in various counties. They stretch from the North of Scotland League to the Cornwall Senior League and many carry minor sponsorships. These range from the Tartan Bitter Trophy in Yorkshire to the Watney Mann Knock-Out Shield in East Anglia. The decision to concentrate on those wholly concerned with our leading cricketers necessitated the omission of three first class tournaments. The first two, as their names imply – Haigh National Village Cricket Championship and the National Club Knock-out Competition – cover an extremely wide range of players. The Cricketer Cup sponsored by Moet and Chandon keeps the old boys of 32 of our most revered Public Schools well aware of 55-over cricket and is most keenly contested.

To all the players, for so much enjoyment, to the administrators for their hard work and particularly to our many sponsors whose financial help has kept the flag flying high on our County grounds, may I propose a hearty vote of thanks.

Jim Laker
Putney December 1976.

One-day Cricket–Good or Bad?

It may come as a staggering surprise to younger readers to learn that 2,200,910 paying customers watched First Class County Championship cricket in 1947. That same year Surrey awarded me my County cap and I embarked on the ten most memorable years of my life. From a professional cricketer's point of view I doubt whether those years could have been bettered. The game was alive with great players and wonderful characters, competition was fierce amongst County professional staff and the Universities produced a whole stream of brilliant cricketers. Each Whit Saturday one joined a mass of supporters walking over Trent Bridge in the full knowledge that there would be a capacity crowd and equally aware that barring mishaps the side batting first would be round about the 400 mark by the close of play. Moving south to the Oval the needle game with Middlesex would produce another full house and a similar situation would reveal itself in Yorkshire and Lancashire.

Just look at the facts and figures in relation to Surrey games against Middlesex around that time

1949 – 51,250 spectators paid £4441
1950 – 58,530 spectators paid £4326
1959 – 45,000 spectators paid £4800

and these figures do not include several thousand members. Let us swiftly compare three identical fixtures during the last ten years.

1972 – 1933 spectators paid £682
1973 – 2354 spectators paid £1002
1974 – 1401 spectators paid £586

Every keen observer has his or her own theories to account for the dramatic fall in attendances at County cricket matches and on reflection one can only conclude that it was never one prime factor but a combination of many. There were those who lay the blame solely on the shoulders of the players themselves but this I believe to be grossly unfair. In part they could share the blame for as the situation grew more desperate it seemed to me the players, by adopting ultra cautious methods when a more positive attitude was vital, contributed latterly towards the decline.

The slump really began when the field of entertainment widened considerably, and preference for playing and watching other games took over. Golf, tennis and squash drew thousands away from cricket, more people took up angling than ever before, swimming and athletics increased in popularity, and probably most important of all, sales in the motor car business rocketed. Our roads over the week-end were jammed tight with families making their way to the nearest seaside resort – families who years before had spent their leisure hours watching County cricket. Year by year the counties were slipping further and further into the red and needed more than members subscriptions to stay afloat. I mention this simply because the cost of membership had been kept at a ridiculously low figure during the times of plenty. As a full member with many counties you could watch at least fifty days championship cricket for around £3 per season. Progressive increases over these years would not have caused the present day outcries when counties now really need one hundred per cent increases to help keep them solvent.

M.C.C., all be it in good faith, looked at means of brightening the game. They introduced shorter boundaries, limited the number of leg side fielders, awarded bonus points for batting and bowling and restricted the first innings in a county match to 100 overs. Such measures have had little material value and have served only to make the game even more difficult to comprehend. The situation was critical and without exception each and every county was in dire financial difficulties. The fact that they are still in business today is due solely to the increase in one-day cricket and the coverage given to the game by B.B.C. Television. It has surprised me that so many people whose living has depended upon the survival of the game have continually been amongst limited-over cricket's most severe critics.

On the other hand the B.B.C. was quick to appreciate the impact of the one-day game and it is indicative of its support that during the normal season around 31 days are given to coverage on limited-over cricket. Obviously there are advantages; plenty of action with faster run scoring plus wickets falling at regular intervals; bigger crowds giving greater atmosphere and, with a fair percentage of the games being played away from normal venues, greater scope for the imaginative producer to incorporate many delightful panoramic shots. Most important of all the viewer can be certain of a definite result before close down. Regular television visits to the counties has been the reason for the growth of advertising signs around the grounds and these contracts would not have been renewed unless the advertiser believed that there was a real chance of the cameras being present. By and large the B.B.C. has accepted this situation, though it still will not condone or agree to the practice of the sharp salesman covering the boundary boards with a temporary sign for a one-off promotion. Thus, if one takes into account the sponsorship and advertising fees which have benefitted the counties as a result of television, plus the hundreds of thousands of pounds paid by the B.B.C. for the right to cover and consequently help to popularise one day cricket, television's contribution has been a vital one.

Finally to substantiate the financial benefit to the counties of one-day cricket the following figures taken from the balance sheet of Surrey County Cricket Club in 1974 represent conclusive proof of why the one-day game has been the saviour of the counties.

T.C.C.B.

Share of Tests, Gillette Cup, Benson & Hedges and John Player League	£30,508
Sponsorship and advertising	£17,343
	£47,851
County Match Receipts	£16,768

A further breakdown shows home gate receipts as follows:

11 Home 1-day Games		11 Home County Championship Games	
(11 days cricket)	£9609	(33 days cricket)	£5831
Average daily gate	£874	Average daily gate	£177

If anyone believes that these are loaded figures purposely illustrated to add weight to the one-day argument, I am certain that similar research undertaken with a northern county such as Lancashire would show an even more startling difference. The new competitions have unquestionably brought the crowds back to our grounds and have helped to give the game a new following. Membership opinion generally is split down the middle – those who believe it to be great entertainment and those who will not tolerate it at any price. The first section continue to turn up regularly in strength whilst a good percentage of the second group sit through the afternoons to make sure they are not losing out on their membership fee. It would be interesting to do a survey of new members who join a county with one-day cricket as their priority. Of even more interest is the make up of the public who attend Gillette, Benson & Hedges, and the John Player League. They certainly cannot be there in appreciation of the true arts and finer points of the game of cricket which are conspicuous by their absence, but they come along in good numbers to see more positive action than is apparent in the three-day game. They know that at the end of it all there will be a result and on the way home they can look back and possibly discuss the match in its entirety. There is no similar satisfaction for them in spending four hours at a three-day county game of 18 hours duration. I suppose that it is something akin to arriving at a soccer match 20 minutes after the start and leaving 25 minutes before the final whistle. Mention of soccer reminds me that Lancashire have managed to attract several thousand young supporters of Manchester United F.C. to limited-over cricket at Old Trafford, and they have certainly made their presence felt. There is little likelihood of their appearing at an Old Trafford Test Match.

Turning now to the actual game of cricket itself, where, if

at all has one-day cricket exerted a good influence? First and foremost the standard of outfielding has improved out of all recognition, and in reaching such a high peak proves conclusively that the present day cricketer is fitter and more athletic than his counterpart of bygone days. There was a time when the cricketer would continue playing until he was about ready to drop and the Club had no alternative but to end his contract. In those days it was always possible to hide a couple of fielders and the slips and gully provided a ready-made haven. Even in my playing days I can never recall going through any serious form of physical training which is now an accepted part of pre-season build up. I was certainly fit enough to bowl 40-over spells and complete 1500 overs in an English season which would shatter one or two bowlers at the moment.

Having said that there is no doubt that neither I nor my colleagues would have stood up to the physical demands of the one-day game without attempting to put a much finer edge on our accepted degrees of fitness. Having watched the likes of Keith Boyce, Peter Lever, Geoff Arnold sprinting out to a boundary cutting off the ball a yard short of the line and disappearing into the crowd makes it hard to believe that I could ever have seen Alf Gover, Alec Bedser or Stuart Surridge in similar circumstances. Still one cannot lose sight of the fact that afternoon cricket calls principally for the containment of batsmen and of denying their every possible run, whereas in earlier years one had to dismiss batsmen to win matches and, even if on occasions it meant sacrificing runs to do so, it was often a gamble well worth the taking.

So often if the game of cricket wins on the one hand it loses on the other and if our one-day cricket has been responsible for a raising of standards in outfielding, should it take the blame for the falling standards in close to the wicket catching? With fewer opportunities for the slip fielders, in particular, to practice the art of close catching we seem to be dropping more catches close to the wicket in Test cricket.

It was most noticeable during M.C.C.'s Tour of Australia in 1974/5. Australians, Mallett, the Chappell brothers and Walters who play very little one-day cricket held some of the most spectacular catches I have ever seen; in comparison I was unable to single out even one of England's slip fielders who looked in the same class.

And now, what of the batsman and the one-day game. In May 1969 I had some pretty scathing remarks to offer on television with regard to an innings played by Glenn Turner of Worcester in a John Player League match at Northampton. Northants batting first had made 174 off their 40 overs on a pretty good wicket. A useful, but certainly not a match-winning score, when Worcester had Headley, Graveney, D'Oliveira, Ormrod and Hemsley in good striking form. Glenn Turner, then 21 years old and starting his second full season, came in first and unaccountably remained there for close on 30 overs during which time by means of a few defensive pushes here and there he accumulated 22 runs. This innings, if so it can be called, completely finished any Worcester's hopes of victory and, notwithstanding a few late sixes from D'Oliveira they could manage only to total 108 with 4 wickets still in hand. I am certain that this innings was the turning point in Glenn Turner's career. He was a young, extremely ambitious, serious, dedicated batsman with an excellent defence and intelligent enough to appreciate that to reach the very top he must start to play some shots. One-day cricket was to be an admirable platform for him. He was hardly likely to be condemned on a Sunday afternoon if it meant a few failures and he quickly set about increasing his stroke play. The possessor of one of the straightest bats in the game of cricket, he matched his wits against defensive fields, proving that runs could be scored in the most pleasing style without resorting to the vagaries of the old 'heave-ho'. Glenn, who these days quite rightly takes his place amongst the top half dozen batsmen in world cricket, has long since admitted the debt he owes to limited-over cricket and there are several others who have benefited by it.

Dennis Amiss, Richard Lumb and Turner's New Zealand colleague John Parker have all become better players and have carried their free scoring habits on into the more serious games.

Let me then briefly sum up the good effects of one-day cricket. It has brought the crowds back to our cricket grounds. Bigger gate receipts and the support of sponsorship, advertising and B.B.C. Television have bolstered the critical financial position of the counties, helping to subsidise three-day County cricket, our real training ground for Test match cricketers. It has been instrumental in setting outfielding standards at a higher level than ever before and has been of the utmost value in improving the stroke play of many of our leading cricketers.

Having made out a case in favour of one-day cricket then let us explore the factors which have had an adverse effect on first class cricket in general. For a change let us start with the bowlers.

It used to be common practice in all forms and grades of cricket to bowl on and outside the off stump to a predominently off-side field whenever a bowler was looking to try and keep a batsman quiet. In the days when it was every young batsman's ambition to perfect the off drive, cover drive and cut, the bowler could successfully block the shot and the method paid off. With slower pitches and the new-found ability of many batsmen to manoeuvre the ball from outside the off stump through the vacant gaps on the on-side the bowlers in turn had to change their ideas. As a result the most effective type of bowling from the faster men and the medium pacers is that which delivers the ball, well pitched up around the leg and middle stump. With so many batsmen already moving into line there is positively no way in which they can hit the ball through the covers and the cut shot has just about disappeared from their repertoire. They are therefore, committed to try and force the ball away through the on side (now more heavily populated) and indeed only the very best batsmen have ever had the ability to find the leg-side gaps.

One-day cricket, therefore, has produced a breed of accurate medium pacers solely reliant on length and line which is all very well, though extremely tedious to watch. They pay their way handsomely when bowling 8, 11 or 12 overs and invariably collect cheap wickets towards the end of the innings when batsmen in desperation are swinging across the line of the ball. Further they build up reputations, particularly on Sunday afternoon, which makes many people wonder why they are not considered when international sides are selected. Not only would they come down to earth with a bang in Test cricket but they are hindering the progress of the attacking bowler, be he paceman or spinner. I offer no criticism to captain, selectors or the bowler himself, for in a game offering greater financial rewards for winning teams, I too would select my most effective bowler.

As you might expect I feel extremely sad at the gradual disappearance of the spin bowler from first class cricket and have no hesitation in saying this sorry state of affairs is almost entirely the fault of limited-over cricket. It saddens to see such a fine leg spin bowler as Intikhab Alam, a rare sight in any case, relegated to the job of deep mid off, middle order batsman and rarely given a chance to show his undoubted skills with the ball. Before anybody leaps on my back and cites Derek Underwood as one of the most successful bowlers in any form of cricket I would respond by saying that I do not put him in the category of slow spin bowlers, nor indeed would I include that prolific wicket taker Don Shepherd. The chief survivors have been the old hands, those with sufficient experience to adjust to the methods required and most obviously include Norman Gifford, Ray Illingworth, Brian Langford, Fred Titmus, John Mortimore, Peter Sainsbury, Bob White and Lance Gibbs.

The Lancashire pair of Jack Simmons and David Hughes, along with Leicestershire's John Steele, also have good records but all three can make runs which provides added security. Pat Pocock by greatly increasing his pace has become an integral part of the Surrey one-day attack but I cannot help feeling it has had a detrimental effect upon his performance in County Cricket. It is hoped the same does not apply to Middlesex's Phil Edmonds. My sympathy for Intikhab extends to Jack Birkenshaw and Bishen Bedi, both considered good enough to go on tour with their country yet unable to command a regular place in limited-over cricket. Thus by a process of elimination we are left with only two spin bowlers brought up in one-day cricket who have managed to weather the storm. Ray East of Essex and David Graveney of Gloucestershire are well established and may shortly be joined by Phil Carrick of Yorkshire. They really are to be congratulated on coming out on top with the odds so heavily stacked against them.

One of the few joys of retirement from cricket is that as the

years go by people are apt to remember your better days and
forget completely the bad ones. As a result, I am sure that
many cricketers subsequently become in the imagination, far
better performers, than they ever were in reality. I often in
fact wonder whether the great W.G. himself was really as good
a player as most of us have been lead to believe. On many
occasions I have felt distinctly uncomfortable when I hear my
own name mentioned in this context for whereas I am sure I
was a good bowler I still harbour a few doubts as to whether
I was as good as some generous friends would intimate. It
seems that a few others share my view as I am asked periodically how I would have fared in limited over cricket. My young
friend, Pat Pocock, who took over my role as Surrey's off
spinner, has quizzed me many times and he, like others of his
ilk, is anxious to know how I would have bowled to batsmen
chasing runs in a shortened form of cricket. In the golden days
of the late 40's and early 50's a good percentage of matches
played on excellent pitches were won and lost on 3rd day
declarations. Quite a number of sides would have considered
it an insult if they were asked to score at anything less than
90–100 runs per hour. Bearing in mind that the over rate in
those days was around 20 overs per hour, and often more
when the slow bowlers were in action, one was really talking
in terms of five runs per over.

Translated into a Gillette Cup match this would mean 300
runs per innings. One therefore accumulated a fair amount of
experience when it meant bowling to Edrich and Compton or
Simpson and Hardstaff in full flight. The chief difference, of
course, was that the slow bowler would still be looking to take
wickets and win the match rather than adopting a means of
containment and settling for a draw.

Perhaps that is being somewhat evasive and reminds me of
the day I first introduced Micky Stewart to Sir Leonard
Hutton. The young Surrey batsman was seeking some advice
about his own play and Leonard's answer was to explain in
detail the old LBW law at great length!!

On reflection I am sure I would have fared little better than
any other spin bowler if I had started my career with one-day
cricket in full swing. I am equally certain that if I had started
to play afternoon cricket as a fairly experienced campaigner

there would have been no alternative but to quicken the pace, lower the trajectory, change the direction and depend on a batsman's frustration to collect wickets. I would have been good enough to have reasonable success but in truth I believe I would have hated every minute of it. At the outset of this chapter I said I was sure I played my cricket at the best time and to have been forced to dispense with the arts of spin and flight and bowl in a manner described above is, in my view, a prostitution of the slow bowler's craft.

Few people would argue that amongst the limited-over batting stars would naturally appear the names of Richards and Greenidge, Boycott and Hampshire, Turner and Jameson, Edrich and Luckhurst. They have all one thing in common – opening batsmen. The first point to make is therefore that there is really only one place to bat in limited-over cricket and secondly that the middle order batsman is on a hiding to nothing. Talented and experienced players with the confidance and power to overcome defensive field placings have however survived in the middle-order and brought excitement to many a game. Basil D'Oliveira, Jim Parks, Viv Richards and Brian Davison fall into this category and the most remarkable innings I have seen was Davison's undefeated 158 against Warwickshire at Coventry in 1972. He came in to bat when 25 overs had been bowled and during the remaining 30 overs he hammered ten 6's and eleven 4's in a wonderful exhibition of clean hitting. It is a memory to cherish and is the exception rather than the rule in this form of cricket. It is when the responsibility for pushing along the score falls on the shoulders of the promising young player that problems arise. The pressures of trying to establish himself by orthodox means are great in themselves; he is acutely aware of what is required of him but would have to be exceptional to put it successfully into operation. My first sightings of Frank Hayes were three successive one-day innings at Old Trafford. On each occasion he appeared at the crease when Lancashire, after solid starts, needed quickly to improve their run rate. The opposition were equally aware of the position and the seamers bowled accurately and defensively. Stalemate developed and with a big crowd voicing their protests, Hayes, in desperation, swung across the line of the ball and departed crestfallen to the pavilion. Any confidence he had was shattered and however much he may have been persuaded that these failures were of no great consequence to his career it must have had repercussions in the more serious games that followed. Whilst I agree that the arrival of too many overseas cricketers has retarded the progress of our own young middle order batsmen the one-day game, which for our counties occupies anything between 21 and 27 games of cricket per season, must also take a fair share of the blame.

One of the most difficult and trickiest tasks in our game is the compilation of the annual fixture list. Years ago we were concerned only with three-day county cricket, five Test matches, University and school cricket and a few M.C.C. games. Even then consideration had to be given to traditional holiday fixtures and availability of grounds but even so when the pattern had been set it was not unusual to see Yorkshire finish a game at Bradford on Tuesday afternoon and be due to play Kent at Dover on Wednesday morning. This might well be followed by a 350-mile dash to Scarborough on Friday evening for another Saturday start.

Today there has to be incorporated into the County fixture list, 16 Sunday games, together with Gillette and Benson & Hedges matches, and one wonders how much the extra travelling now necessary adversely affects the players performance in one-day cricket. The 40-over game on Sunday is a particularly difficult problem as apparently it is impossible regularly to coincide the Sunday fixture with the County match taking place over the weekend. Of course it does happen on occasions, but a county like Glamorgan have often to undertake a considerable journey to fulfill their Sunday fixture. A batsman who has spent most of Saturday at the wicket and who contemplates a full day in the field on Monday is less than likely to be alert both mentally and physically on Sunday under these sort of conditions.

Such a situation occurs less frequently in Gillette Cup cricket though several of the rounds immediately follow a Test match. Thus it is quite likely that at the conclusion of a Manchester Test several players may have long journeys to make in time for an early start the next day.

My own experience was that a hard Test Match with all the

obvious pressures usually leaves one much less than 100 per cent in mind and body and it takes a day or two to recharge the batteries. Great Test performances very often are followed by mediocre efforts in a County match. The Gillette Cup is a vital and critical competition which no player can afford to take lightly, which all makes it a tough task for him to retain his form immediately following a Test match.

If one-day cricket has taken a firm hold in this country what then has been the reaction to this competitive form of limited over cricket overseas? Generally speaking it has never been greeted with the same amount of enthusiasm in Australia or the West Indies, both of whom have limited their participation to their own brand of Gillette Cup cricket but on quite a minor scale.

Neither of these countries are dependent on one-day gates to keep them out of debt as neither the States of Australia nor the Islands of the West Indies retain playing staffs or the large clerical and administration staffs necessary for the organisation of full time cricket in our country. Their average spectator goes along to his game in the hope of seeing one of the batsmen make 150 or 200 runs and will equally applaud the sight of the genuine fast bowler coming in off a long run for a final spell late in the day. I have a feeling that a 60-over match in these countries is a little bit of fun for 'them, has never up to now been taken very seriously and in no way would they wish it to interfere with their traditional games of cricket. Many of the Australians have voiced the opinion that the spread of the one-day game in England has been the principal reason for the falling away in standards of our Test match cricketers. If this is so it is vital that we retain our limited-over games in their present form, so should we not be looking for ways and means of overcoming a position which before long could leave us shorter than ever of Test match cricketers? To do this we must first of all realise there is a great difference between the 40-over John Player cricket and the longer versions sponsored by Gillette and Benson & Hedges.

Without wishing to decry the 40-over game, which creates enormous interest and is great fun to be involved with, one cannot escape the fact that it is something of a lottery. As a county captain I would seldom include any of my young batsmen or spin bowlers in the make up of my side and would see that they concentrated their efforts on the 60 days County cricket open to them. Once the batsmen had made their mark they could be drafted into Sunday cricket, preferably in the opening positions. To fill the gap I would be looking for two or three seasoned Club cricketers, of whom there are many, who can bowl accurately for eight overs and play a few shots in the middle of the order with the knowledge that neither their job nor their cricket future would be at risk.

Although the other two competitions constitute a much more acceptable game of cricket I would again be loathe to play a promising slow bowler but would have fewer reservations about including a young batsman. Even so he must be allocated a high position in the order where, in a 60-over game, he has a reasonable chance of playing himself in.

To keep up the flow of future Test cricketers and hope to retain our standards we should ensure that for the younger player, County cricket should have top priority. There are still more opportunities for them in this form of cricket than are available to a West Indian or Australian and we should be grateful to the one-day game for making it still possible.

One final point which appears a constant source of worry to many people. Two out of three of our one-day competitions are sponsored by tobacco firms to the tune of around £175,000 a season. Hanging constantly and threateningly over the heads of our cricket administrators is the fear that the Government may finally decide that tobacco sponsorship of sport is forbidden. If this came to be, would our one-day cricket survive? Fresh negotiations involving amounts of money such as this obviously cannot be easy but cricket remains fairly fortunate that the coverage it receives through television and the national press is probably more extensive than any other sport and for this reason I am sure that several commercial companies would be delighted to get on the band wagon.

As long as one-day cricket is played, arguments will rage long and furiously as to whether it is good or bad for the game itself. Adopting a perfectly selfish attitude and that of a slow spin bowler, I can simply reiterate what I said at the outset of this chapter – I am delighted to have played the game when I did.

Speaking as an inveterate watcher of limited-over cricket and as a full time commentator it has, and I hope will, continue to give me immense satisfaction and enjoyment. The game has always been bigger than the individual and if the limited-over game has been good for cricket to the possible detriment of some cricketers, perhaps therein really lies the answer.

Gillette Cup

For as long as the game is played, cricket will owe an enormous debt of gratitude to Gillette Industries for their courage, foresight and not least the financial support of sponsorship. They brought to our game a completely new dimension at a time when cricket was slowly sinking to its knees – County treasurers were dubious about where next years' salaries would be coming from. Gillette were the leaders in opening up an entirely new vista and inspiring other companies to follow suit and breathe new life into our summer game.

Initially it was far from being an easy path and many diehard members, with cricket history at their finger tips, were quick to point out that a knock out cricket cup had been promoted 90 years earlier by M.C.C. and had been an abysmal failure. The expense of transporting cricketers around the country for a one-day game, and forever the problems of our inclement weather prolonging these matches, with no guarantee of large gates were the obvious drawbacks envisaged by many. There has always been something rather sacrosanct about cricket and I well remember the furore when business agents first appeared on the scene. It seemed almost that cricketers were bringing the game into disrepute by employing a professional man to help in their affairs, though for the life of me I could never understand why, when a theatrical agent had been totally acceptable for so many years. There is no doubt that the M.C.C. were then not quite certain what the effects of sponsorship would be and they approached the whole business with a great deal of caution. In retrospect it is easy to be critical but in those early days how could one be entirely sure that cricket was not selling its soul and in danger of being lost in wholesale advertising and commercialism.

Happily the Gillette Company were not looking for a 'quick buck' and their long and lasting association with M.C.C. has been built on mutual respect, in fact one could honestly say that they have never really cashed in on their cricket sponsorship. They have certainly never attempted to lay down the law as to how the one-day game should be played nor have they ever wished to use facilities of our countless cricket grounds to promote their products.

At a luncheon at Gillette headquarters some time ago I was surprised to hear the results of a market research in relation to Gillette products and cricket. It appeared that after 10 highly successful years of Gillette sponsorship only a relatively small percentage of the public associated Gillette products with cricket's Gillette Cup! It did occur to me a surprising factor that a company which must spend many thousands of pounds on commercial T.V. advertising had never seen fit to incorporate some of our leading cricketers in their T.V. commercials to provide the necessary link. In addition I could see nothing but good for them in undergoing a sales promotion in a large store of a town where Gillette Cup cricket was taking place. I am sure that for a small fee several of our top players would have been only too pleased to put in a personal appearance. It may well be that I am entirely wrong and a good reason why I am not in commercial marketing. On the face of it, therefore, it would seem that cricket has fared rather better than the sponsors, though there can be no question of Gillette being dissatisfied and they have continued to renew their support with ever-increasing stake money.

Not even the most optimistic of the pro-sponsorship group could have foreseen the immense success and pleasure that the Gillette Cup has given over the years, though there was a certain amount of encouragement forthcoming when in 1962 Leicestershire, Derbyshire, Nottinghamshire and Northants combined to run their own Midlands knock-out competition in May of that year. This competition was quickly arranged when it was discovered that these sides had blank dates and they wisely believed they would acquire practical knowledge of a limited-over game in readiness for the Gillette Cup due to get under way 12 months later. The final itself, when Leicestershire beat Derbyshire in a real thriller by only seven runs, allayed many fears and with 493 runs scored in the day without ever making a mockery of the game, the stage was set.

The first Gillette contract was agreed in November 1962. Looking back, the sponsorship figure of £6500 plus a Cup, 'Man of the Match' awards for each tie must now seem a pretty miserable amount. Although thirteen years later the figure has been substantially increased it does not at the present time compare with the larger sponsorship fees coming from John Player and Benson & Hedges. For all that it was Gillette who blazed the trail and for this they surely deserve a little preferential treatment.

The rules of the competition covered just about every exigency and have scarcely needed amendment. Originally the games were scheduled to be of 65 overs per side with a bowler allowed a maximum of 15 but several dusk finishes persuaded the organisers that 60 overs was a more realistic figure with each bowler restricted to a maximum of 12 overs. The one major difference of opinion I have nursed for several years concerns this limit of 12 overs per bowler, although I fully appreciate the thinking behind the strategy. There was always a hidden fear that fiercely competitive limited-over cricket offering handsome rewards to players would be monopolised by defensive attitudes. After all it was reasoned that the best method of containment would be in the hands of the quicker bowlers with the leg stump as their target. Thus it was erroneously concluded that if at least five bowlers shared the attack, the spin bowlers would play their full part. Surely there was no way in which a County side could field five first line seam bowlers. How wrong we all were. I recall in those early days several instances of spin bowlers being immediately omitted and in successive weeks saw G. Boycott of Yorkshire and D. Green of Gloucester, two redoubtable batsmen, putting in a spell of medium paced bowling. Happily this situation has improved over the years and the spin bowlers ration has continued on the up grade. For a long time now I have been opposed to the limitation of bowlers overs as I firmly believe it is totally unfair to penalise a bowler who is doing well. I have seen new ball bowlers of the calibre of Geoff Arnold and Peter Lever reluctantly pulled out of the attack after four or five overs when in great form, in order to be kept in reserve for later batsmen. The opening batsmen themselves are aware of this and the knowledge that they need only weather the storm for a limited period is a comforting one. Nobody has yet suggested in reverse that a top batsman be only allowed a limited time at the crease. It would be interesting to see the reaction of a packed Southampton crowd with Barry Richards in full cry just passing the 50 mark and being greeted over the loudspeaker with 'Come in No. 1, your time is up'. No doubt it would help to re-establish some of our middle order batsmen, but God forbid it should ever happen. Similarly I do not believe it should happen to a bowler.

Gillette Cup in its first year was limited to first class counties in the usual knock out basis but with 17 counties taking part it was necessary to play a preliminary match. It is interesting these days to recall that this took place at Old Trafford between Lancashire and Leicestershire, two counties subsequently due to achieve some remarkable results in one-day cricket. However in 1962 they were the bottom two counties in the championship and it was necessary for one to be eliminated before the Gillette Cup proper was under way. Lancashire were the winners, Peter Marner hit the first Gillette century and became the first 'Man of the Match', the presentation being made by Frank Woolley.

Early Gillette cricket was really all about Sussex who carried off the Gillette Cup in 1963 and 1964 in front of great and enthusiastic Lords crowds. They did not, in fact, lose a cup tie until their 10th game, against Middlesex in 1965. Superbly led by Ted Dexter, who had always been alert to the possibilities of the new venture, they had a fine all round side. Ted has always been a great thinker on the game of cricket and it was obvious from the start that he had quickly stolen a march on his rival captains, setting a pattern in one-day techniques which remained as a blueprint for the game for several years.

In 1964 the competition was enlarged by incorporating the top five sides in the Minor Counties championship the previous season, an arrangement which stands to this day. The introduction of the Minor Counties it was felt would add a real Cup flavour to the competition and the organisers were possibly casting eyes on the soccer scene and thinking in terms of a Yoevil or Wimbledon and the interest that a major upset would cause. The odds against this happening in cricket must remain remote and as the years went by the Minor Counties were simply chopping blocks for the full time players whose batting and bowling performances were enhanced as a result of these encounters. The miracle was finally achieved after 10 years when Durham, in 1973, travelled down to Harrogate and of all sides overcame a full-strength Yorkshire team by five wickets. It was a great occasion, for Durham cricket in particular, but did not represent a change of fortune for the Minor County cricketers who continue to come off second best in what have become by and large one-sided contests. So often the part timers have little opportunity of serious cricket in any quantity early in the season and it is normally August before Minor County cricket really is in full swing. However, I still believe that M.C.C. and Gillette are correct in continuing to include the leading Minor County sides in the competition. The five qualifiers are certain of a reasonable financial hand out when the cash is divided each year on performances. This payment is absolutely vital to many of the sides and acts as a great incentive to qualify in their normal championship programme.

It was a minor county side, Cambridgeshire, who took part in one of the strangest ever Gillette Cup ties which illustrates on the one hand what a bugbear our climate can be, yet on the other how fortunate Gillette have been in limiting farcical games of cricket to the barest minimum. This particular tie between Yorkshire and Cambridgeshire was scheduled to take place at Bradford where no play was possible for three long frustrating days due to heavy rain. Finally it was agreed that the game should take place at Headingley and a few days later the sides returned to Leeds on a bright sunny morning only to find the whole square awash after a thunderstorm overnight. The position was particularly desperate for Cambridgeshire who, as amateurs, with full-time occupations, were limited in the amount of time they could spare for cricket. The Yorkshire secretary began to telephone adjacent grounds for availability and the league ground at Castleford was hard and dry and a 2 o'clock start was definite. A reduced over match would be played. The party moved on only to be overtaken by the Leeds thunderstorm which then quickly reduced the Castleford square to a soggy mess. Undaunted the groundsman went to work and to his great credit produced a playable stretch of turf in time for a 4 p.m. start by which time the 'game' had been restricted to a 10-over slog per side. Under those conditions anything could happen and in fact the first ball of the match sent down by Fred Trueman was hit for a mighty six by David Fairly the Cambridge opener. As the ball was being retrieved the rain came steadily down but the players opted for a soaking provided they could see it through. See it through they did and with most of them saturated to the skin honours could be said to be even. Yorkshire won the match and David Fairly was the proud possessor of the 'Man of the Match' award.

I cannot recall a repeat of Castleford since that day, though heavy rain played a part in a memorable Gillette final at Lords in 1965 when Yorkshire met Surrey and those fortunate enough to be there witnessed arguably the finest century ever made in Gillette cricket. There seemed little prospect of any play at all on Cup Final Day when heavy rain lashed Lords continually on Friday and was still bucketing down late at night. The fine early morning was sufficient good news for a determined effort by Billy Griffith and the Lords' staff, supplemented by further help and drying equipment from the nearby Oval, to salvage a day's cricket and save a disappointing day for the many thousands of overnight Yorkshire travellers. The decision on the starting time was left with the two captains, Brian Close and Micky Stewart. They both appreciated that despite the tons of sawdust which just about obliterated the famous square (apart from a green soggy stretch of 22 yards) it was never really fit for a 12 o'clock start, and were reluctant to commit their teams to such hazardous conditions. However the gentlemanly persuasion of the M.C.C. secretary and the vociferous advice from supporters won them over and on a day when both captains would have been happy to lose the toss, it was Micky Stewart who had to make the decision. Instead of going down in history as an utterly unselfish batsman and a brilliant close catcher who more than any cricketer I know, put the game of cricket far

ahead of personal achievement, Micky will be remembered as
the skipper who put Yorkshire into bat in the 1965 Gillette
Final. Many years before in this same ground the story goes
that a very youthful Brian Sellars put M.C.C. in to bat on a
sodden pitch without consulting the senior Yorkshire professionals. As M.C.C. passed the three figure mark without
loss Sellars was asked by one of his elder statesmen, 'What
ever made thee put 'em in?'. 'My father thought it was the
right thing to do,' replied Sellars. Quick as a flash came the
response 'If I were thee I'd go get thee Dad to bowl 'em out
then!'

There was, of course, reasonable justification in Stewart
asking Yorkshire to bat. The saturated pitch was hardly likely
at any stage to become really difficult (which in fact proved to
be the case) and as the day progressed the outfield should dry
appreciably. No one could possibly have foreseen that that
September day would produce an individual innings of sheer
magic from the bat of Geoffrey Boycott. A first wicket partnership of 192 with Brian Close, who made a masterly 79,
finished the game as a contest and Yorkshire's final total of
317 for 4 in 60 overs remains the highest ever for a Gillette
Final. Boycott occupied the crease for a shade under three and
a half hours for his 146; an innings which no one could
possibly forget included three sixes and fifteen fours, made
against a fine all round attack on a pitch and outfield which
few considered fit for cricket. Boycott had shed all his inhibitions, had played with confidence and complete freedom from
the start and produced a range of strokes which few players of
any era could have rivalled. Probably most important of all,
he had given a perfect illustration and final proof that success
in limited-over cricket can be achieved just as well by the
matured stroke player.

If Boycotts' performance that day stands supreme in my
memory one cannot easily forget the great impact that the
mighty Clive Lloyd has made at Lords, nor the brilliance of
Asif Iqbal in coming within a whisker of giving Kent victory.
Mike Procter and Tony Brown in turn had it seemed the
whole of Gloucestershire on their feet with memorable batting
exploits. The Finals by and large have been dominated by the
batsmen who have revelled in the good fortune of so many

gloriously hot September Saturdays. The bowlers have had to remain contented with secondary honours and for a spectacle such as this the balance has been a good one. It has produced year after year a days cricket unparallelled in terms of the limited-over game anywhere in the world and has firmly established Gillette Cup Cricket as the premier competition in the eyes of all who follow the game.

It would be quite wrong to close this chapter without mention of the one person who has been chiefly responsible for the enormous success of Gillette cricket from its very conception. Gordon Ross, author and journalist has been sporting Consultant to Gillette Industries for the past 25 years and a man it seems who has worn a path between Arsenal F.C. and Lords via the R.A.F. Club in Piccadilly. His administration over this period of time has been completed without a blemish and the Gillette Cup under his guidance, like the carnation in his buttonhole, has continued to flourish. In recent years he has helped to introduce Gillette cricket in both South Africa and the West Indies, a task in itself which must speak volumes for his personal tact and diplomacy. At the time of writing and just having returned from the West Indies where the first Gillette Cup winners were Barbados one sensed something of a lukewarm reception for instant cricket. Perhaps the older followers, still re-living the triple centuries amassed by their beloved Weekes, Worrell, Walcott and Sobers are viewing this newfangled cricket with some degree of suspicion that caused so many of our own revered members to doubt the wisdom of it here 15 years ago.

In a changing world it seems a safe bet that it will be accepted and enjoyed at Kensington Oval, Barbados, just as it is at Kennington Oval, London S.E.11.

Gillette Cup Rules

Duration   One innings per side, each limited to 60 overs.

Hours of Play   Normal hours to be 11 a.m.–7.30 p.m. Semi-finals and Final to start at 10.30 a.m. though the umpires may order extra time, if, in their opinion, a finish can be obtained. The pitch to be completely covered in the event of rain.

1   Batting is a lonely job in 'one-day' cricket!

2   But not so in a Test match.

3   Keith Boyce – King of the John Player all-rounders.

4 and 5 Collecting Gold Medals has become a habit for
Lancastrians Barry Wood and Clive Lloyd.

6   Clive Lloyd – is there a more powerful bat in cricket?

7   *Right, above*   Glenn Turner – is there a straighter bat in
    cricket?

8   *Right*   A team of eminent judges.

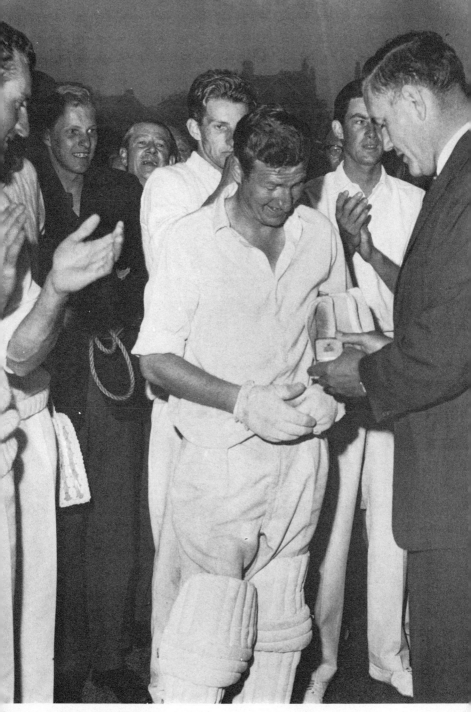

9 *Left* Up from Somerset, and 10 Down from Leicester.

11 *Above* Sussex led the way in the Gillette.

12 Lancashire – took a firm grip.

13 With apologies to Victor Sylvester.

Limitations of Overs by Any One Bowler   No bowler may bowl more than 12 overs in an innings. If due to the weather in the Cup Final the duration of each innings is reduced to 50 overs no bowler may bowl more than 10 overs.

A Tie   In the event of a tie, the result will be decided in favour of the side losing the lesser number of wickets. If both sides have lost the same number of wickets the winner will be the side with the highest score after (i) 30 overs, or if still equal (ii) after 20 overs, or if still equal after (iii) 10 overs. In the event of both sides being all out, in or under 60 overs, the overall scoring rate of both sides will be the deciding factor.

Past Winners

1963	Sussex beat Worcestershire by 14 runs
1964	Sussex beat Warwickshire by 8 wickets
1965	Yorkshire beat Surrey by 175 runs
1966	Warwickshire beat Worcestershire by 5 wickets
1967	Kent beat Somerset by 32 runs
1968	Warwickshire beat Sussex by 4 wickets
1969	Yorkshire beat Derbyshire by 69 runs
1970	Lancashire beat Sussex by 6 wickets
1971	Lancashire beat Kent by 24 runs
1972	Lancashire beat Warwickshire by 4 wickets
1973	Gloucestershire beat Sussex by 40 runs
1974	Kent beat Lancashire by 4 wickets
1975	Lancashire beat Middlesex by 7 wickets
1976	Northamptonshire beat Lancashire by 4 wickets

Highest Innings Total   371 for 4 off 60 overs
Hampshire v Glamorgan (Southampton) 1975

Lowest Completed Innings Total   41 off 19.4 overs
Middlesex v Essex (Westcliff) 1972

Highest Individual Score   177 C.G. Greenidge
Hampshire v Glamorgan (Southampton) 1975

Best Bowling Analysis   7 for 15 A.L. Dixon
Kent v Surrey (The Oval) 1967

John Player League

The inauguration of the Gillette Cup had whetted the appetites of the cricket followers for one-day cricket but it seemed that M.C.C. in the sixties were slow to appreciate the impact of this sort of cricket. On the other hand the Bagenal Harvey Organisation, through its Founder, immediately saw a new vista on the horizon – one-day sponsored cricket played on the most obvious day of the week, with the possibility of T.V. coverage. It had to be an instant success, which indeed it was and ran for four seasons before M.C.C. finally realised the potential of Sunday cricket and brought their full powers to bear. Working in close co-operation with John Player Ltd and the B.B.C. they founded what is now known as the John Player League and to all intents and purposes the Rothman Cavaliers went quickly out of business.

Not for the first time in my life I found myself in a difficult position. An original member and player of the Rothman Cavaliers and subsequently a commentator on these games, I was also an honorary life member of M.C.C. and under contract with the B.B.C. Together with Denis Compton and Godfrey Evans I had been an early client of Bagenal Harvey with whom I had a close association. I knew him very well, had always found him to be fair and understanding and consequently was appalled to hear the criticism levelled at him so often by people who would not have recognised him if they had passed him in the street. It seemed that the principal accusation was that Bagenal was feathering his nest, making a huge personal profit out of the Cavaliers and cricket in particular, whereas the money should be going back to the game itself. There is no denying that Bagenal Harvey is essentially a business man, shrewd and successful and I am sure that for four years at least he made a profit to which he was entitled in view of the time, thought and the total administration undertaken on behalf of the Cavaliers. Certainly the profit margin never approached the exalted figures banded around in some cricket circles as a closer inspection would have confirmed.

To begin with the games against the Counties were played when possible to augment the benefit of the player granted a testimonial, and one can readily recall sums of £3000 handed over to players like Tom Cartwright and Ken Taylor after games at Edgbaston and Huddersfield. It is as well to recall that in those days this sort of figure was normally as much as some cricketers could expect from a full year's benefit. Similarly further matches were played in aid of national charities and furtherance of cricket in many different ways. The players who represented the Cavaliers were household names in the game of cricket and nowhere else in the world was it possible to turn out on a Sunday afternoon such a talented array of International stars.

A typical Cavaliers XI in the late sixties would include Denis Compton, Godfrey Evans, Tom Graveney, Fred Trueman, Ted Dexter, South Africans, Graham Pollock and Denis Lindsay, West Indians Gary Sobers, Clive Lloyd and Lance Gibbs plus Bobby Simpson from Australia. All these cricketers were paid realistic fees for their services which, added to travelling and hotel expenses, made the outgoings substantial to say the least. On more than one occasion the Cavaliers invited and paid the air fares of promising overseas cricketers to give them an opportunity of experience in the very highest of company and of course it all required full time organisation and administration to arrange a full season's cricket. No one was likely to undertake this on a voluntary basis.

Over three years a sum of just under £10,000 was handed over to M.C.C. as a donation from the Cavaliers. To offset the high expenditure there was of course the payment made by the sponsors Rothmans and the B.B.C. but in those early days these sums bore no comparison to sponsorship and television money paid at present. When in fact the Cavaliers decided to continue their programme after the start of the John Player

League, using local weekly sponsors, but without television coverage, they went quickly into the red and were disbanded proving surely that the profits of the golden era could never have been as substantial as many people believed.

On one issue there could never have been any doubt or argument. The entertainment value of Cavalier cricket was superb. Almost without exception each and every one of these International stars maintained their own very high standards and as a result the crowds flocked to see them. Many of the better features of our game, which have subsequently been lost in the present day interpretations of one-day cricket, were there in abundance. The pace bowlers set attacking fields and it was not uncommon to see leg spinner Bobby Simpson and off spinner Lance Gibbs in action together bowling reasonably lengthy spells. Denis Compton reproduced some vintage performances from the past, Godfrey Evans astonished the crowds with his long-kept brilliance and agility and who could fail to appreciate the artistry of a Sobers, the power of a Dexter and the elegance of a Pollock. A young star, Clive Lloyd, gave evidence of great deeds to come and nobody really cared if every now and again a hint of stage management crept in to ensure the public were totally satisfied. It is therefore not surprising that up and down the country so many people mourned the passing of the Cavaliers.

However one could readily understand the feelings of many M.C.C. committee members. Attendances at first class matches had begun to fall dramatically, playing staffs had been seriously pruned in an effort to meet the wage bill and cricket had again begun to struggle for its very existance. Suddenly an outside organisation had formed their own competition which was immediately successful, exhilarating to watch and financially sound. Although there were benefits forthcoming to M.C.C. and several leading cricketers as a result of Cavalier cricket it was patently obvious that if M.C.C. were to sit down and organise a Sunday competition on a national scale, involving every county playing each Sunday, plus substantial sponsorship and television coverage, they were sure to be on a winner. They were also bound to have the support of the counties, for whereas the Cavaliers were attracting an average gate of say 10,000 per Sunday with their solitary fixture, this weekly estimate could be multiplied eightfold if all the counties were involved each week and the financial benefits would obviously be much greater. So M.C.C. went to work and unfortunately there followed a good deal of ill feeling between Bagenal Harvey Organisation and the M.C.C. Bagenal felt that having organised and successfully promoted Sunday afternoon cricket, he was very shabbily treated by the powers that be at Lords, yet on the other hand M.C.C. were fully justified in going ahead with their plans which would ensure an essential income for each and every county. It seemed a pity to me that it was not possible for everyone concerned to sit round a table and work out an amicable solution. There were many, myself included, who remained sympathetic to the Cavaliers cause, yet felt equally that if cricket were to overcome its present financial difficulty, it had to be left to the governing body of cricket to take over the formation of the new Sunday League. I supported John Arlott in his view that the Cavaliers XI should be added to the odd number of 17 counties to make up exactly nine fixtures per Sunday and the televised match each week would be the one involving the Cavaliers. As the years have now gone by I am now not convinced it would really have been practical. M.C.C. decided there could be no compromise and a clean break was the only answer. To further their point they refused to allow any contracted first class player to appear in any match for the Cavaliers. This had the effect of drying up the supply of talent. The original sponsors, Rothmans, had become utterly disenchanted with the whole turn of events and withdrew their sponsorship for ever and a day from the game of cricket. The Cavaliers faded into oblivion.

Details of the new Sunday competition were announced in readiness for a start to be made in 1969. M.C.C. had accepted a generous offer of sponsorship from another tobacco company, John Player & Son, though the Players League as it was originally known was something of a misnomer. It appeared that the majority of people were of the opinion that this was a new league organised by the players themselves! The company moved sharply to put matters right and the accepted title of the John Player League left no one in any doubt as to the sponsors.

The new competition could not in fact have had a more dismal start. The rain fell steadily through May, only five of the 30 County Championship matches produced a result and the touring West Indies side sat huddled in pavilions up and down the country. Sunday cricket was badly hit and 12 matches were totally abandoned due to rain. Warwickshire were the chief sufferers with exactly one-quarter of their programme washed out. The Midlanders appeared to have the ideal combination with such fine strikers of the ball as Bob Barber, Jim Stewart, Rohan Kanhai, Mike Smith and John Jameson. Their attack, spearheaded by the king of medium-paced seam, Tom Cartwright and Test bowlers Dave Brown and Lance Gibbs, seemed a likely combination. It was Lancashire whose only bleak day was the Roses match in August who eventually ran out as first year winners. The combination of their overseas stars, Lloyd and Engineer and the League experience of the home-bred players paid early dividends and there was no doubt that they were the first County to come to terms with the requirements of 40-over cricket. One would have thought that their great rivals Yorkshire, whose players without exception had come through the training ground of competitive Saturday afternoon, limited-over league cricket, would have been in contention. However they could only finish half way down the final league table and the reason put forward by their captain Brian Close seemed to suggest a disenchantment with this new game of instant cricket. It is interesting to note that the full batting averages in this first year were headed by two 20-year-olds – Peter Willey of Northampton who averaged 45, and Greg Chappell, then of Somerset, who averaged 38. I have for long held the opinion that if Peter Willey had been born in Australia he would have become a fully fledged Test cricketer long ago!

The first season was bound to have its teething troubles and they were around in plenty. The limitation of the bowler's runs up to 15 yards threw our real pace bowlers out of their stride and it is significant that John Price could finish only 28th in the final averages with John Snow and Peter Lever way below in 44th and 45th position respectively. At the head of affairs was Tom Cartwright and occupying second position was the medium pacer Roger Knight, then of Surrey. More worrying still was that David Green of Gloucester and John Sullivan of Lancashire were in fourth and fifth positions. Even their greatest admirers would find it difficult to justify their claim as even an occasional change bowler in a first class match.

Over the years, both Snow and Lever, have been able to adjust successfully to the abbreviated run up, but has limited over cricket been a reason for the shortage of genuine pace bowlers at present? It cannot have helped, for whilst one remains critical of pace bowlers embarking on a long and needless run, one has to be something of a freak to generate real pace with only a 15-yard run up. Sunday cricket remains the forte of the accurate and too often defensive-minded medium pacer.

Too many of the batsmen believed the game demanded an all out attack from the start with too much reliance placed on a frantic chase for boundaries. It was quite astonishing to find early batsmen holing out at mid off and extra cover in the first five overs of an innings. Indeed it took some little time for counties to discover the art of pacing the innings. Lancashire, who in 1970 retained the title were the acknowledged masters in this art, placing importance on a good start over the first 10 overs, steady acceleration through the next 20 and then with wickets in hand, to be in a position for an all-out assault in the closing overs. Figures reveal that to begin with bowlers, due to the batsmens' lack of experience had the upper hand. In 1969 only one batsman could average over 40 whilst 11 bowlers finished the season with wickets captured at a cost of less than 14 apiece. In six years the picture had been completely reversed. By this time 11 batsmen averaged over 40, whereas only one bowler was able to pick up wickets at a cost of under 14 each.

How had the cricketers themselves reacted to the new competition? After speaking to players in all parts of the country it seemed to me that they were, by and large, not particularly enamoured but were quite willing to reserve a final opinion until a later date and give the competition a chance to settle down. The present-day cricketer is much more commercially minded than those of the last generation and many of them harboured doubts as to whether their share of the sponsorship money was a realistic one. The total sum, reported to be in the region of £90,000 (which included £3000 to each county) was a generous one but if a side did not finish in the top three which carried rewards of £1000, £500 and £250 respectively, it seemed that they would receive only what the County could afford to pay them, plus £50 shared amongst the team for each victory. In 1969 Sussex recorded only three successes which meant that their efforts over 16 weeks were rewarded by £150 shared by at least 16 players, considerably less than £1 per man per week. Perhaps a little cynically captain Micky Stewart tossed the ball to Geoff Arnold in an early Surrey fixture which had involved a 200-mile round trip plus 30 overs from the pace bowler the previous day with the words, 'Give it all you've got for the next four overs, three quick wickets and we will all be £4 better off.' Happily, since those days the crowds have flocked to Sunday matches, gate receipts have exceeded even the most optimistic budgeting and conse-quently the Counties have been abe to pay the players a realistic fee for their Sunday efforts.

As the years have gone by the earlier doubts in the minds of the players seem largely to have vanished and the competition has continued to increase in popularity, though I believe that they still regard it as less worthwhile than the two other major limited-over competitions.

One particular grouse has remained throughout the eight years and this refers to the problem of travel. The gruelling part of Sunday cricket is often not so much the actual playing but the travelling backwards and forwards to fulfil the fixture. Apparently it is not possible always to combine the three-day County weekend fixture with John Player matches on the Sunday and consequently some rugged journeys are called for. A typical situation arose last season when Glamor-gan were engaged at Worcester on Saturday, Monday and Tuesday and had to play Essex at Colchester on the Sunday. Which ever way you look at it a return journey of something like seven hours must take its toll.

The same County were seriously handicapped a couple of years previously when after spending a full Saturday in the field at Cardiff they were called upon to drive to Buxton in

Derbyshire. Arriving in the early hours of Sunday morning and aware that the same journey lay ahead of them that evening, it is little wonder that they had no great appetite for that particular John Player fixture. These are by no means isolated examples and when one considers the thousands of miles that are driven by weary cricketers in hot weather, it has been a miracle that there has not been more serious accidents. Motorway driving requires a fresh and clear mind combined with 100 per cent concentration.

Searching for further incentives John Player introduced from the outset a batsman's pool of £1000 per season with one share of the pool for each six hit. Similarly for the bowlers an equivalent sum was set by to be shared by bowlers taking four wickets or more in a match. The dividends have varied only slightly from year to year with the average reward for each six standing around £2.50 whilst the successful bowlers have pocketed about £17 each time they have managed to take four wickets. There have not been too many Gloucester or Surrey batsmen playing in the vast acres of Bristol and the Oval amongst the recipients and if the scheme is loaded in favour of the players playing regularly on the smaller grounds, it would be impossible to organise it in any other way. At least for a change the bowlers it would seem, have a better chance of coming out ahead financially of the batsmen.

With the sponsors providing these various tit-bits the B.B.C. felt it too should be involved and offered a prize of £250 for the fastest 50. Keith Boyce was the first to collect, racing to the half century in 23 minutes. It was subsequently agreed that the award would relate only to televised matches and the fastest 50 judged on balls received rather than on time taken. The first stipulation was open to comment but the second a more sensible suggestion as it was possible for a player to spend 15 minutes in the middle without ever receiving a ball. The record at the moment is held by Majid Khan who in 1975 hit 50 off 22 balls for Glamorgan against Northants at Wellingborough. It had to be the easiest £250 Majid has ever collected. The game itself was a complete farce with Majid and company smashing the friendly spin of Mushtaq and Steele to the tune of 77 from eight overs during a match played completely out of character with normal Sunday routine. When the B.B.C. withdrew, John Player supplied the extra prize, but, remarkably, the prize is still restricted to televised games.

The rules of this competition have not changed despite several worthwhile proposals which have been recently put forward. A statement issued from Lords at the end of 1975 stated simply that it would be foolish to amend the rules of such a highly successful promotion. I find this hard to accept, for whereas I agree that the John Player League has indeed been a top class innovation, I am equally convinced that one should not believe that it cannot be improved. Take for instance a situation which now occurs almost every Sunday concerning field placing when the side batting second is chasing runs over the last half dozen overs. Quite frankly it becomes a bore now to see the entire fielding side placed on the boundary edge. If the ground is anything like a respectable size the chances of the batting side have become negligible and the whole scene looks more like the Dodgers searching for a home run in the Yankee stadium.

I feel strongly that a rule should be incorporated into the competition to ensure that at all times there should be four fieldsmen in addition to the bowler and wicket keeper within 30 yards of the pitch.

We have been extremely fortunate in the last few seasons not to have witnessed very many of the 10-over 'slog' matches. Once again I firmly maintain that it is both totally unfair and degrading to watch first class cricketers attempting a result when the sides are allowed 30 minutes each. If it is not possible for the teams to play at least 20 overs per side then it should go into the record books as a 'no result' match with each side taking two points.

Thirdly an element of quite unnecessary gamesmanship has been patently obvious in relation to over rates. At the moment the rules state that a new over cannot be commenced after ten minutes past 4 o'clock and if by that time say only 38 overs have been bowled and the side batting first are not all out, then the match is reduced to one of 38 overs per side. Consequently there have been cases of teams who due to injury, Test calls etc, find themselves short of a bowler of sufficient quality to make up the requisite number of overs and purposely slowing down the over rate allows their fifth-choice bowler to bowl only five or six overs. Consider the position of the batting side who realise that they are not going to receive their full quota of overs. They have the choice of trying to push the scoring rate along with the possibility of losing wickets in the process and at the same time making sure they are not bowled out thereby giving the fielding side, who have purposely slowed down the over rate, the full 40 overs to make the required runs. Perhaps the people concerned may look a little deeper when the next season's rules for the John Player League are reviewed.

Having offered these criticisms let me emphasise that in no way do I belong to the brigade of cricket fanatics who spend their time ridiculing the John Player League. They are a hard core who still dream of 20,000 people at a County match watching the Hobbs and the Woolleys, the Mays and the Comptons and yearning in vain for the return of the leg spinner.

Whilst I will always freely admit that there are many occasions when I find it extremely difficult to look seriously at some of the Sunday games, one cannot argue against the fact that they bring a great deal more entertainment to a far greater number of people than do the majority of three-day matches. In an era when everyone has such a wide choice of spectatorship the thousands of people who arrive at Canterbury, Hove, Leeds and Old Trafford early on a Sunday morning complete with deck chairs and packed lunches, would not be there if they did not believe they were getting full value for their money. There are far more people who enjoy the action of 400 runs being scored from 80 overs in four hours' non-stop cricket than the comparative few who watch the leisurely activities on a County ground in mid week.

If John Player gates have doubled since 1969 then the viewing figures on B.B.C.2 have quadrupled over the years. One cannot forget the many thousands who for a variety of reasons are unable to watch cricket from a ringside seat. No one would have dreamt 20 years ago that it would be possible to watch a game of cricket in your own lounge from beginning to end on a Sunday afternoon from a perfect vantage position and if you should happen to be in doubt as to a batsman's dismissal, then the action would be replayed again for you in slow motion. During the first seven years of the competition there were probably only half a dozen of the 17 counties who had mastered the techniques of 40-over cricket. Lancashire, Kent, Worcestershire, Leicestershire and Hampshire were always to be found in contention and if Essex had been able to show a little more staying power throughout August, they would have added a new name to the list of winners.

As I have constantly held the opinion that 40-over cricket must always be something of a lottery this feature of John Player cricket has continued to surprise me. We had in fact to wait until 1976, the eighth season of the competition before we had a situation which I had envisaged arriving years before.

With only three Sundays to complete the season only four points (ie one victory) separated 13 of the 17 Counties. Eight Counties were joint leaders with 32 points and another five close behind on 28. That shrewdest of captains and cricketers, Ray Illingworth, summed up the situation as it stood at the time. 'When the John Player League began, a few teams picked up the technique quickly, others struggled to master the unique demands of the 40-over game. Now everyone has the ability and experience to play the Sunday game well. I saw this situation coming and said at the start of the season that any side would be capable of beating any other. This has been borne out by what we have seen. There was no better illustration than the victory by Gloucestershire, who were bottom, over Essex, who were top. Consequently you just cannot predict results any more.'

The situation was in fact so tight that Illingworth's own County, Leicestershire, who at that stage were one of the joint leaders, could either finish as outright winners of the League or, if they lost these last two matches, could end the season in the bottom half of the table.

By the time the final Sunday of the season (5th September) was reached five Counties stepped out with a mathematical chance of ending the day as John Player League champions. Somerset with 40 points were the obvious favourites as their fixture was against bottom club Glamorgan at Cardiff (but heed Ray Illingworth's warning above). Sussex also with 40 points and a final game at Birmingham would obviously be champions if they could beat Warwickshire and Glamorgan could surprise Somerset. However if both Somerset and Sussex collected the points the first deciding factor is the number of away wins, but both sides would again be equal with five each and then the decision will go to a run rate over the season and in this respect Somerset had a clear advantage. If, however, both Somerset and Sussex were to lose, Kent, Essex and Leicestershire were hovering hungrily on their heels. Of these three Kent playing Gloucester at Maidstone had the best run rate, Essex playing Yorkshire at Leyton could be champions with most away wins and outsiders Leicestershire could even pull it off provided all the other Counties lost and their batsmen ran riot at the Oval.

It was vital at the end of such a pulsating season that the television cameras should be at the ground where the championship would be finally resolved, yet there was no way on earth that all five games could be covered. What a situation facing series producer, Bob Duncan! After long hours of consultation we finally decided on the following. A full unit would be installed at Birmingham with John Arlott as commentator. B.B.C. Wales would in any case be covering the Glamorgan v Somerset fixture with commentary in the capable hands of Ossie Wheatley and Wilf Wooller. Just in case the two favourites should fall I was to accompany our ace B.B.C.1 producer, David Kenning, to Maidstone with just two cameras to provide interim reports. John Phillips back in Television Centre in London would attempt to co-ordinate the afternoons' production. To complete the picture John Player had their helicopter based at Pebble Mill, Birmingham, engine running ready to transport Peter Walker and the trophy to Cardiff or Maidstone at a minute's notice should the championship go to Somerset or Kent.

By tea-time there was only one certain outcome of the games. Kent batting first had taken the Gloucester attack apart at Maidstone. Woolmer and Tavare scoring at seven runs an over had paved the way for a brilliant Asif century which included the fastest televised 50 off 39 balls and a final total of 278 for five. Their victory was assured. At Edgbaston, Sussex had been bowled out for 149 by Warwickshire and it seemed that they would have to produce a superhuman effort to stay in contention. Glamorgan batting first at Cardiff had scored 191 and this game was really wide open with Somerset desperately needing a good start in their effort to clinch the title.

No decision could yet be taken on the helicopter route but with Warwickshire apparently coasting to victory a decision could not be delayed for too long. Flying time to Maidstone, the longer of the two trips was one-and-a-quarter hours which meant a deadline of about 5.15 to 5.30 p.m.

The news from Cardiff looked bad for Somerset when they lost their first three wickets for 27 with Denning, Close and Botham all back in the pavilion. Now it seemed that Kent was likely to collect the trophy once again and Bob Duncan with fingers tightly crossed sent the helicopter complete with John Player official, Peter Walker, en route to Maidstone. Of course no sooner had they departed than Somerset staged a glorious counter attack through Brian Rose and those redoubtable pair of Somerset batsmen Mervyn Kitchen and Graham Burgess. So well did they play that 64 runs were needed off eight overs with six wickets in hand. In the meantime Kent had overcome Gloucestershire by 123 runs and as the first bottles of champagne were opened the helicopter appeared over the lovely Mote ground and dropped on a perfect length on the recently vacated pitch. But had they come even now to the wrong ground? Back at Cardiff Graham Burgess was still dealing every kind of hammer blow to the wilting Welsh attack and Somerset needed 18 to win off two overs. Ten were needed from the final over, four were needed off the final ball. In fact three for a tie would be sufficient but alas for Somerset they could manage only two and the greatest cliffhanger in John Player cricket saw Somerset fail to win the championship after four months cricket by the margin of a solitary run. Although I was fortunate enough to witness it all at Maidstone, and delighted to have made the correct choice, I would dearly have loved to have seen Somerset prevail. What a wonderful double that would have been with Northants collecting the Gillette Cup on Saturday and Somerset the John Player League the following day. Essex in the meantime had beaten Yorkshire at Leyton and Leicestershire had taken the points from Surrey at the Oval which finally left the top five positions as follows:

	P.	W.	L.	Pts.	Away wins	Run Rate
Kent	16	10	6	40	5	4.988
Essex	16	10	6	40	5	4.560
Leicestershire	16	10	6	40	4	—
Somerset	16	10	6	40	4	—
Sussex	16	10	6	40	4	—

Thus Kent by the narrowest of margins collected £2500 prize money whilst the £1250 runners-up prize and the £500 for the third place was to be shared by the other four Counties, giving them £437.50 each. Essex firmly believed that if the title could be won on the number of away wins, the runners-up position ought to be determined in exactly the same way and they should in fact receive £1250. In many ways one could readily appreciate their argument and they must have felt that the fates continually conspired against them. Back in 1971 they had lost the title to Worcestershire by 0.0037 of a run and the finest mathematical calculations. On the other hand cast a thought for unlucky Somerset. If Essex were given the runners-up position they could reflect they would receive only a little over £100 and they too were within a single run of being champions. One finally hoped the T.C.C.B. would recommend an increase in cash rewards as compensation for the four Counties.

So ended the greatest ever season of John Player League cricket, a competition which has grown in strength, has been a life saver for each and every county and even if it can never satisfy the purists, it will continue to bring great enjoyment and entertainment to countless thousands in the years to come.

John Player League Rules

Duration of Matches   Matches will consist of one innings per side. Each innings is limited to 40 overs. If the team fielding first fails to bowl 40 overs by 4.10 p.m. the over in progress shall be completed. The innings of the team batting second shall be limited to the same number of overs. If bad weather delays the start of the first innings or suspends the length of either innings, the number of overs will be re-arranged so that each side bats for the same number of overs.

Bowling   No bowler may bowl more than eight overs and the length of a bowlers run-up is limited to 15 yards, measured from the wicket.

Result

i   A result can be achieved only if both teams have batted for at least 10 overs, unless one team has been all out in less than 10 overs or unless the team batting second score enough runs to win in less than 10 overs. All other matches in which one or both teams have not had an opportunity of batting for a minimum of 10 overs shall be declared 'No Result' matches.

ii   In matches in which both teams have had an opportunity of batting for the agreed number of overs (ie 40 overs each, in an uninterrupted match, or a lesser number of overs in an interrupted match) the team scoring the higher number of runs shall be the winner. If the scores are equal, the result shall be a 'Tie' and no account shall be taken of the number of wickets which have fallen.

iii   If the team batting second has not had the opportunity to complete the agreed number of overs and has neither been all out, nor has passed its opponents score, the following shall apply:

a) If the match is abandoned before 6.40 p.m. the result shall be decided on the average run-rate throughout both innings.

b) If, due to suspension of play, the number of overs in the innings of the side batting second has to be revised, their target score shall be calculated by multiplying the reduced number of overs by the average runs per over by the side batting first.

iv   In the event of the team batting first being all out in less than their full quota of overs, the calculation of their average run rate shall be based on the full quota of overs to which they would have been entitled and not on the number of overs in which they were dismissed.

Points Winning team gets four points. In the event of a tie each side gets two points. In a no result match each side gets two points. In the event of two or more teams finishing in first position with an equal number of points, their final positions will be decided (i) the most wins or, if still equal (ii) the most away wins or, if still equal (iii) the higher run rate throughout the season. Teams finishing equal second or third shall be considered as such and share the prize money.

Past Winners

1969	Lancashire	49 points
1970	,,	53 ,,
1971	Worcestershire	44 ,,
1972	Kent	45 ,,
1973	,,	50 ,,
1974	Leicestershire	54 ,,
1975	Hampshire	52 ,,
1976	Kent	40 ,,

Highest Innings Total   307 for 4 off 40 overs
Worcestershire v Derbyshire (Worcester) 1975

Lowest Innings Total   23 Middlesex v Yorkshire (Leeds) 1974

Highest Individual Score   155 not out B.A. Richards
Hampshire v Yorkshire (Hull) 1970

Best Bowling Analysis   8 for 26
K.D. Boyce Essex v Lancashire (Manchester) 1971

Career Records 1969–1976 (compiled by Bill Frindall)

MOST RUNS		*Runs*
1	B.A. RICHARDS	4270
2	B.W. LUCKHURST	3395
3	M.J. SMITH	3349
4	G.M. TURNER	3336
5	R.G.A. HEADLEY	3273
6	G. BOYCOTT	3193

MOST WICKETS	*Wickets*
1 J.K. LEVER	171
2 K.D. BOYCE	170
3 D.L. UNDERWOOD	169
4 S. TURNER	164
5 R.D. JACKMAN	157
6 J.C.J. DYE	152

MOST WICKET-KEEPING DISMISSALS	*Dismissals*	*Ct*	*St*
1 R.W. TAYLOR	145	113	32
2 G.R. STEPHENSON	130	99	31
3 R.W. TOLCHARD	129	114	15

MOST CATCHES BY NON-WICKET-KEEPERS	*Catches*
1 R.M.C. GILLIAT	56
C.T. RADLEY	56
3 M.H. DENNESS	54

MOST APPEARANCES	*Matches*
1 S. TURNER	124
2 J.K. LEVER	122
3 J.A. ORMROD	120
G.R. STEPHENSON	120
5 D.P. HUGHES	119
E.W. JONES

John Player League Double The following six cricketers achieved the double of 1000 runs and 100 wickets in the least number of matches:

Keith Boyce (Essex)	51 matches
Graham Burgess (Somerset)	71 ,,
John Shepherd (Kent)	74 ,,
Stuart Turner (Essex)	78 ,,
Tony Greig (Sussex)	80 ,,
Trevor Jesty (Hampshire)	80 ,,

Benson and Hedges Cup

There can hardly have been a better day's cricket since the Benson & Hedges Cup was first introduced, than the two semi-finals played on June 23rd last year. They were, in fact, two local derbys with Surrey v Kent locked in combat at the Oval and Worcestershire providing the opposition at Edgbaston. On both grounds the sun shone fiercely down on ideal batting pitches and in the two games a total of 1094 runs were scored in front of large and enthusiastic crowds. This indeed was one-day cricket at its very best.

Kent batted first at the Oval where Mike Denness led the way with a dashing century. Graham Johnson and Asif Iqbal both completed 50's and Surrey were left with the improbable task of scoring 281 in 55 overs to go through to the Final. Geoff Howarth and Chris Aworth saw them well on their way with a fine opening stand of 92 but without any real support from the middle order it seemed their outside chance of victory had gone when the seventh wicket went down with the score on 218. They were not done for yet, thanks to a fine innings from young David Smith and solid support from Robin Jackman. These two in fact took the score on to 261, just 20 more required, three wickets in hand and four overs left. Suddenly it was anyone's game until Derek Underwood re-appeared in the attack. He had previously accounted for Howarth and Intikhab and now within the space of a few balls, he clean bowled Smith, took a caught and bowled to get rid of Jackman, induced Arnold to give a catch to Denness and Surrey were all out for 264, just 16 runs adrift. Underwood, with 5 for 35 on a batsman's day, must have been unlucky to miss the Gold Award which was presented to Denness.

At Edgbaston Worcestershire were pleased to take first strike and reached 80 before Alan Ormrod was bowled. If they were despondent at losing D'Oliveira very cheaply there was ample compensation in a delightful display from Imran Khan who made a sparkling 72.

For all that it was the run-hungry Glenn Turner who gave yet another masterly exhibition of cultured stroke play in carrying his bat for 143. At the end of 55 overs Warwickshire were faced with the monumental task of scoring 282 to win. Neither Jameson nor Amiss managed to settle and D'Oliveira took both their wickets but Rohan Kanhai was perfectly at ease and was beginning to bring back memories of earlier years when Paul Pridgeon took a wonderful return catch and Warwickshire were in trouble. Abberley and Humpage did not help the cause and at 164 for 6 it seemed all over bar the shouting. Bill Bourne and Eddie Hemmings had different ideas, attacking the bowling with good judgment in a partnership of 68, but on their departure at 232 the task of collecting another fifty runs was always out of the reach of David Brown and company. They still had one wicket intact when the 55 overs were completed and the losing margin had been whittled down to a mere dozen runs. Two great games and it was almost uncanny how much they resembled each other.

There was nothing quite as thrilling as this in the Final which was a repeat of three years earlier and the margin of Kent's victory this time was almost identical. Kent, put in to bat, made 236 and despite this being the highest total yet in a Benson & Hedges final, one felt it was still within the range of Worcestershire. Unhappily for them Turner, Ormrod and Khan had left their runs at Edgbaston and the sponsors were indebted to Basil D'Oliveira for making something of a match of it. Crippled with a torn hamstring and no mobility whatsoever he could only stand stock still and swing the bat. He did this to such effect that he numbered a six and five fours in his courageous 50 before departing to the biggest ovation of the day. The Gold Award, quite rightly, went to Graham Johnson, not only for his top score of 78, but for four outfield catches. Thus the Benson & Hedges Cup concluded another successful year and ended a competition now firmly earmarked in the cricket calendar at Lords and one which has gone from strength to strength since its inception in 1972.

It was in 1971 that Gallaher Ltd., the parent company of Benson & Hedges, were looking very closely at their sporting commitments and fortunately deciding to extend them further. They had just appointed Peter West's company of West and Nally as their public relations consultants, so it was not altogether surprising that the game of cricket was high on their sponsorship programme. It must be extremely difficult to determine the comparative value of sports sponsorship. Is there more mileage in the advertising and public relations world in, for instance, the £50,000 sponsorship of the Eclipse Stakes at Sandown Park or is there better value in putting £40,000 into a golf tournament in Yorkshire?

Although there is a certain amount of pre-publicity on a big race and a huge following in this country, one cannot escape the fact that the event is completed in approximately three minutes. A golf tournament does at least spread itself over four days, but surely neither of these great sporting attractions can compare seriously in value to the sponsor as the game of cricket. The present Benson & Hedges Cup is spread over a period of exactly 12 weeks and is covered not only nationally but locally in the Press almost daily. Most important of all these games receive at least 24 hours of television coverage which means something in excess of 12 million viewers. With these kind of facts to support him together with the increasing success of the Gillette Cup and John Player League, Peter West could not have been unduly pressed to sell the idea of a new sponsored cricket competition to Benson & Hedges. They readily agreed to give it a try and arrived at Lords with a plan formulated.

I first met Peter the best part of 30 years ago, when I seem to recall him working on Radio Luxembourg and sharing an office with Gordon Ross with whom he was involved in editing, producing and publishing the original Playfair magazine. It is a matter of interest and coincidence that these two have played a leading part in helping to establish two of our most successful cricket competitions.

Back at Lords it was agreed that cricket could stand a third one-day competition and after a number of meetings the format was approved by all parties concerned. To avoid any clash with the Gillette Cup, the new Benson & Hedges Cup would be played in the first 12 weeks of the season culminating in a Lords Final before the Gillette Cup was seriously under way. Searching for a competition that would give more variety to the season and wishing to avoid a sudden-death knock-out situation which would not be of much financial aid to more than half the counties it was resolved to go ahead on a similar basis to the present soccer world cup.

It was decided that the country would be split into four zones with five teams taking part in each zone and each side playing each other. The top two teams in each zone would then go forward to the quarter finals and the Cup concluded on a knock-out basis. The matches were to be of 55 overs per side with no bowler allowed to bowl more than eleven. A Gold Award, to be judged by a former Test cricketer, would be presented at each game to the outstanding cricketer. The total sponsorship fee paid by Benson & Hedges was the very generous figure of £80,000, of which £16,000 would go in prize money to teams or individuals. Little wonder the Benson & Hedges Cup was greeted with enthusiasm, particularly by the players.

I was slightly disappointed with the decision to limit the game to 55 overs, as opposed to 60 overs, but it seems that this was done as a variation to Gillette rules. Also what a good opportunity it would have been to forget about limiting the number of overs per bowler, thoughts on which I have enlarged upon elsewhere. It also has taken a little time to educate people in talking in terms of the Gold Award rather than the Man of the Match. Again the sponsors were searching for a difference which has now become accepted and is in line with their general advertising theme. Selection of the zones and sides to compete has, I suppose, been the major problem and talking point and one which even now has not been successfully solved. With 20 sides required and the first-class Counties providing 17 there were three vacancies. Originally Oxford and Cambridge universities played in alternative seasons but after three years and 12 matches they had managed only one victory. Since then they have combined their resources and consequently met with greater success culminating in a fine win over Yorkshire in 1976 at Barnsley.

Unhappily the Minor Counties who filled the final two places have had a completely disastrous five years. Changing their titles from Minor Counties North and South to Minor Counties East and West has made not the slightest difference and their record to date is – played 40 and lost 40! They are at an immediate disadvantage when the games are played so early in the season and few of their players have had the chance of regular practice. A more obvious reason for their poor showing is the fact that all the zonal fixtures are played on a Saturday, the one day of the week when they cannot call upon so many of the professionals within the county who must fulfil their contract with their various Club sides. It is hard to believe that in the future one could happily anticipate any change in their affairs but it is equally difficult to offer an alternative. One suggestion was to incorporate Scotland and Ireland and whilst one could argue that they might provide tougher opposition to the counties, the problems of travel and overall cost in an already busy season seem to rule out the idea.

The original make-up of the zonal sides seemed logical and helped to ease the costs of travel and accommodation but further inspection would show for instance that the South Zone brought forward a particularly strong group of Kent, Essex, Middlesex, Surrey and Sussex. With only two to go forward to the quarter finals, three useful sides were out of the competition. By contrast it seemed that in the North Zone Lancashire and Yorkshire would be almost certain to qualify before a ball was bowled. Derbyshire and Nottinghamshire were in the doldrums and little hope was given to Minor Counties North who made up the quintet. This state of affairs existed for the first two seasons when Middlesex volunteered to leave the South Zone to move into the Midland Group in an exchange with Cambridge University. Strange to relate both sides lost all four matches that year and in 1975 went back to their original zones.

1975 also saw Surrey and Minor Counties (South) on the move in an effort to even out the competition, but it was not until 1976 that a really positive step was made. The decision to scrap the geographical zones and replace them with zones A, B, C and D was a good one. It added greater variety to the season and gave a new and more interesting fixture list. As it stands at the moment the sections are as follows:

A)   Warwickshire, Lancashire, Derbyshire, Glamorgan, Hampshire.

B)   Leicestershire, Worcestershire, Gloucestershire, Middlesex, Minor Counties (W).

C)   Nottinghamshire, Essex, Northamptonshire, Middlesex, Minor Counties (E).

D)   Kent, Surrey, Yorkshire, Sussex, Combined Universities.

All of this shows that M.C.C., Benson & Hedges and Peter West have continually been aware of the original shortcomings, have not spared themselves in efforts to improve the standing of the competition which as a result has shown a marked improvement year by year.

The Benson & Hedges Cup has been dominated by three Counties, Leicestershire, Kent and Worcestershire, despite the success of Surrey in 1974 and the appearance at Lords of Middlesex the following year. In five years Leicestershire have appeared in three finals, winning two of them and Kent have a 100 per cent record at Lords, winning in 1973 and 1976 when on both occasions Worcestershire were their opponents.

Over the next few seasons, I believe, the scene will change just as it has done in the John Player League. With the advance of counties such as Northants, Nottinghamshire and Somerset to mention but three, one can foresee some titanic struggles in the sectional games. Possibly those teams going on to the quarter finals will be qualifying even more often on a superior striking rate. For the first time, last year, there was a near-capacity crowd for the Final and whilst there will always be one or two counties who could almost fill Lords with their own supporters, one would like to think that Benson & Hedges will emulate Gillette and the final will be a sell out before the public are aware who the finalists are to be.

Having spent some time talking to our cricketers on the various one-day competitions, it was interesting to note that the majority seemed to find the Benson & Hedges Cup as the most attractive. To them it combines two very essential issues. They feel that 55 overs constitutes a reasonable game of cricket and they do at least have a chance to play something like a rational match and, more important still, the financial rewards offer a greater incentive to the individual than Gillette or John Player League. In common with our nation as a whole, money has become an overriding factor to our cricketers and who can blame them. Bigger rewards are there for the taking in Benson & Hedges cricket.

Since the rewards naturally depend on results, it is interesting to compare the financial position in 1976 between non-qualifiers Sussex and Kent, the champions. Taking for granted the accepted rule these days that all individual winnings are pooled, Sussex would have benefitted solely to the extent of £200 for one league victory plus £60, the result of two Gold Award wins, both credited to John Barclay. Kent on the other hand, began with three league wins worth £600 and collected another £300 as Team of the Week. In the course of their seven games their players picked up six Gold Awards to the tune of £375 added to which was the major award of £3000 for winning the Cup. A grand total of £4275 in addition to the match fees paid by the County. It is not surprising that our players regard this competition as something very much worthwhile.

Despite its popularity with the players and the watching public, serious doubts about the value to English cricket as a whole are regularly expressed by a third section of cricket's supporters. This group contain those who believe that our ration of one-day cricket was sufficient with the established Gillette Cup and John Player League and that the introduction of yet more limited over cricket has had an even more detrimental effect on first-class cricket. They argue that the Benson & Hedges Cup, which occupies to begin with the whole of May, has severely restricted the amount of three-day cricket available to our players prior to the first Test.

I am sure that those who argue these points have a good case but I am equally sure that the answer would be to re-arrange our first-class County programme in conjunction with the Benson & Hedges Cup as outlined in the final chapter of this book. No less an authority than Mr. E.W. Swanton expressed his views in a television interview from Canterbury last year. Whilst being deeply appreciative of Benson & Hedges he too held the view that the present arrangement severely depleted our early season three-day programme and suggested an alternative form of sponsorship. Our County championship has never been the subject of a serious sponsorship offer – which does not surprise me in the least. Mr. Swanton offered the thought to Benson & Hedges that they may consider transferring their money and affection to the County Championship – suggesting a play-off between the top four clubs each year with the winner becoming the champions for the particular year. This may solve a few cricket problems but as a commercial proposition it had little or nothing to offer a company, a conclusion swiftly reached by several Benson & Hedges executives. I suppose somewhere along the line there is a price for the sponsorship of our County Championship but in view of the general lack of support it engenders and the total absence of television coverage, it must remain a very doubtful quantity for a sponsor. It could never command the £100,000 per annum at the moment tossed into the cricket kitty by Benson & Hedges. It can be estimated that to support a sponsorship of this nature costs half as much again, and thus for an outlay of £150,000 a year on cricket, any company has a right to expect the best possible returns and as things stand at the moment Benson & Hedges seem well satisfied with the present format.

Over the last five years one has grown to appreciate the very professional manner with which both Benson & Hedges and West and Nally have organised and carried through their cricket sponsorship. There never has been the slightest hint that their promotion has in any way devalued our game. The generosity of their hospitality to players, officials and the media generally could hardly have been bettered, and most of all they have introduced into our cricket calendar a competition which has grown in stature and one which I trust will remain for a long time to come.

Benson and Hedges Cup Rules

Duration   One innings per side, each limited to 55 overs.

Hours of Play   Normal hours to be 11 a.m. to 6.30 p.m. with a 2 p.m. start if Sunday play is necessary. The pitch to be completely covered in the event of rain. No bowler may bowl more than 11 overs in an innings.

A Tie If the sides finish with the same total, the side taking the greater number of wickets shall win. If both sides are all out, the side with the higher overall scoring rate shall win. If the result cannot be decided by this criteria, the winners shall be the side with the higher score after 30 overs. If still equal then after 20 overs. If again equal after 10 overs.

Zonal Grouping Five teams play in each of four zonal groups. Each team plays the other in its zone on a league basis. Three points are awarded to the winning team and in the event of a 'no result' match, one point to each team. The two top teams in each zone go through to the quarter finals, from which stage the competition is conducted on a knock-out basis. If two or more teams in a zone have equal points, their final positions are determined on the faster rate of taking wickets in all zonal matches. This is calculated by dividing the total balls bowled by the number of wickets taken.

Past Winners
   1972   Leicestershire beat Yorkshire by 5 wickets
   1973   Kent beat Worcestershire by 39 runs
   1974   Surrey beat Leicestershire by 27 runs
   1975   Leicestershire beat Middlesex by 5 wickets
   1976   Kent beat Worcestershire by 43 runs

Highest Innings Total
   327 for 4 Leicestershire v Warwickshire (Coventry) 1972.

Lowest Innings Total
   62 Gloucestershire v Hampshire (Bristol) 1975.

Highest Individual Innings   173 (n.o.) C.G. Greenidge
   Hampshire v Minor Counties (South) Amersham, 1973

Best Bowling Analysis   6 for 27 A.G. Nicholson
   Yorkshire v Minor Counties (North) Middlesborough 1972

Prize Structure

Champions	£3250
Runners-up	£1600
Losing Semi-Finalists	£1100
Losing Quarter Finalists ..	£650
Winners of each zonal match ..	£220
Team of the week (zonal) ..	£325

Gold Award for Best Individual Performance

Zonal	£35
Quarter Final	£70
Semi Final	£80
Final	£175

Thus over £22,000 of the £110,000 sponsorship fee paid by Benson & Hedges goes in prize money to the players.

Prudential Cup Cricket

I cannot recall any other sponsored cricket occasion which caught the public's imagination more than the Prudential Cup of 1975. From start to finish it was blessed with ideal weather and if, due to the make-up of the competition, there were a few one-sided contests, there was also an abundance of top-class matches which will linger in the memory for a long time to come. Quite apart from the lift it gave to the game of cricket, I am sure it gave some just and overdue compensation to the sponsors themselves. For the previous three seasons the company had ploughed substantial sums of money into cricket in their sponsorship of the Prudential Trophy. These games were played on a 55 overs per side basis by England against the touring sides of 1972, 1973 and 1974. Unfortunately they were scheduled to take place immediately following a tough Test match series and as a result became something of an anticlimax. Consequently one was left in some doubt as to how seriously they were taken by the participants. If one reaches a stage when one-day cricket is not played in a competitive manner then it can rapidly develop into a shambles.

England's second game against Pakistan at Birmingham in 1974 was a great disappointment to all who had the misfortune to be there. If these games could have been played as a prelude to a Test series on grounds such as Hove, Ilford, Southport or Scarborough as opposed to recognised Test venues, I am sure they would have had a great deal more appeal and been all the more successful for it. The Prudential have been perfectly charming hosts and no one could have been more delighted than our cricket authorities when they agreed to take over the sponsorship of this much-vaunted World Cup of 1975.

The idea of a world cup played along similar lines to soccer, involving the leading cricket countries had been on the agenda for some little time. The principal problems were finance and availability.

The generosity of the Prudential to the tune of £100,000 together with anticipated substantial gate receipts appeared amply to cover the costings. With South African cricket still in the wilderness and no prospect of their making the tour to England in 1975 we had the ideal slot in the middle of the summer to cover the fifteen matches necessary to complete the competition in exactly two weeks. It also meant that as the Australians would be one of competing countries it might be possible at the end of the competition to persuade them to stay over for a shortened tour and play a four-match Test series throughout July and August. The very presence of Lillee and Thomson would create great interest and happily the Australian Board of Control agreed to the suggestion.

The requirements for the competition were eight countries split into two groups of four with each side playing three matches within their own group. Four points were to be awarded for a win and if due to bad weather no result was possible over the three days allocated to each game, then each side would collect two points. Play was to commence at 11 a.m. under Gillette type rules, ie 60 overs per side with no bowler allowed more than 12 overs. The two top sides in each group would go forward to the semi-finals with the top team in group A meeting the second team in group B. The major problem now to be decided concerned the countries who would take part. England, Australia, West Indies, New Zealand, Pakistan and India would naturally be here in strength and after what could only have been a fairly lengthy debate Sri Lanka and East Africa were also invited to take part.

From a cricketing point of view it was unfortunate that South Africa were again boycotted as their presence with their wealth of cricket talent would have given the two groups the fine balance that was perhaps lacking. Sri Lanka have been making steady progress towards top International status and their claim to take part was far stronger than any of the other outsiders. The distinct 1000/1 shots were East Africa whose participation I found to be more than puzzling. The difference between the Test cricketer and the weekend player is immeasurably greater than one finds in soccer, for whereas there is always a possibility that over a limited period of 90 minutes Wimbledon will hold the mighty Leeds or the USA will overcome a full strength England side, the odds of this happening in cricket become astronomical. The three results of East Africa's venture into the top bracket confirm this:

1 New Zealand 309 for 5 East Africa 128 for 8.
   Lost by 181 runs.
2 East Africa 120 India 123 for 0. Lost by 10 wickets.
3 England 290 for 5 East Africa 94. Lost by 196 runs.

It also seemed to me that the East Africans used their invitation to reward a number of senior cricketers for service to their domestic cricket rather than selecting one or two of their younger and more promising cricketers. In fact only four of their 14 players were under 30 years of age, two of whom, namely Frasat Ali and Sam Walusimba showed a fair amount of promise. Surprisingly they did not consider for selection three of their countrymen resident in England. Solanky (Glamorgan), Basharat Hassan (Notts) and Owen-Thomas (Surrey) who would certainly have given them experience and greater strength. If, in the future, South Africa are still not to be considered when this competition is repeated, I would greatly favour the host country being permitted to include an 'A' eleven which would add to the interest in addition to providing a large financial saving.

It was with a great deal of anticipation that the draw for the two groups was made and someone unkindly suggested there had been some sticky fingers at Headquarters when England appeared in Group 'A' along with East Africa, India and New Zealand. At least the home side appeared certain of a place in the semi-final. Thus the second group 'B' was a formidable one of Australia, Pakistan, West Indies and Sri Lanka and one could look principally to this section for the really plum games during the first 10 days.

The West Indies were established as firm favourites which was not surprising in view of their great array of talent. Clive Lloyd, the captain, supported by Kanhai, Fredericks,

Greenidge, Kallicharan and Richards gave them a formidable batting line up. All-rounders Julien and Boyce, speedsters Roberts and Holder, spin from Gibbs and a top-class wicket keeper/batsman in Deryck Murray meant that it would take a fine side to lower their colours. England were by no means out of it provided they were able to forget their humiliating defeat at the hands of Australia a few months earlier. It was always possible that Lillee and Thomson in particular might well be tamed by our slower pitches and no doubt the home side had far more experience of one-day cricket than even their most serious rivals. In this respect it was felt that even the mighty Australians may be lacking. There is a world of difference between playing a five-day Test on a hard responsive Sydney wicket and 60 overs at Headingley and the Oval. Their great pace attack would only have 24 six-ball overs between them!

Although drawn in the most difficult group, the team that I had a sneaking regard for was Pakistan. The previous summer they had overwhelmed England, in both Prudential Trophy matches. One would be fortunate to see a better hundred than that made by Majid at Trent Bridge whilst Asif Masood and Sarfraz had ripped the English batting wide apart at Edgbaston. With Majid's support coming from the attractive blades of Sadiq, Mushtaq, Asif Iqbal and the new and exciting Wasim Raja, I could foresee a few surprises in store.

In their usual unobtrusive manner New Zealand too could not be discounted. To be led for the first time by the wonderfully consistent Glenn Turner they were able to reflect on their recent success in the Australasian Gillette Cup and no Kiwi that I have met would sell his wicket cheaply.

Along with England they seemed fairly certain to qualify for the semi finals.

The very make up of the Indian team immediately placed them at a disadvantage. Without even a single top class seam bowler and possibly only Engineer, Gavaskar and Viswanath likely to make any impact with the bat in a limited over game the odds were heavily stacked against their survival. The same could also be said of Sri Lanka though the progress they had made in recent years would surely be watched with great

14 Gloucester shine, having won the Gillette final in 1973.

15   The author at work.

16   *Right, above*   The Benson & Hedges gold award.

17   *Right*   Benson & Hedges final 1975, between Leicestershire and Middlesex.

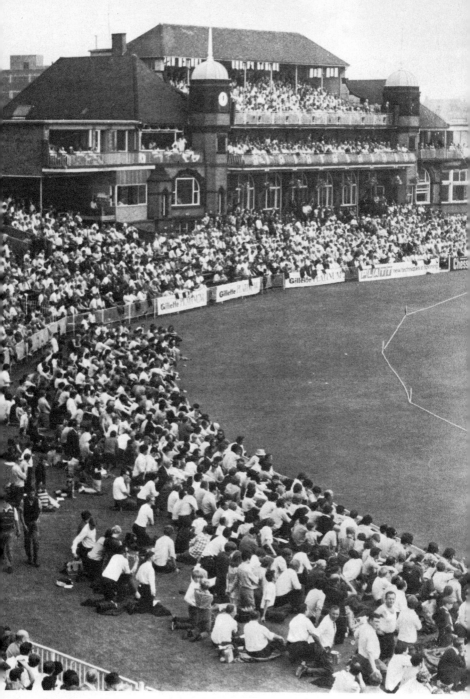

18 Typical Gillette scenes at Old Trafford.

19 Roy Fredericks hooks Lillee for six?

20 Fredericks, hit wicket bowled Lillee!

21 Rohan Kanai. Brilliant, exciting, undeniably one of the 'greats'.

interest. Away from the cricket itself my most treasured memory of the summer was a wonderful reception given at Lords to welcome each and every cricketer taking part. Never had cricket's headquarters seen the like of it before. Every top cricketer in the world gathered under the same roof with a common bond between them all. As I drove slowly home contemplating on what a memorable occasion it had been I could not help but reflect once again on the absence of South Africa's cricketers. Their very presence on such an evening intermingling with the representatives of India, Pakistan and West Indies would have shown once and for all that apartheid does not exist on or off the field as far as the game of cricket is concerned.

Saturday, June 7th dawned bright and clear and the great new adventure was under way. At Old Trafford the West Indies destroyed Sri Lanka by nine wickets and had pocketed their four points by 3.30 p.m. It was a similar story at Birmingham where New Zealand overwhelmed East Africa where Glenn Turner's undefeated 171 was 43 more than the East Africans could muster in total.

Twenty thousand people paid £19,000 at Lords to see England run out easy winners against India. An Amiss century and a flurry of runs from Fletcher and Old gave England a run rate of five-and-a-half runs per over and established a new record score in a 60-over match. In reply the Indians utilised their full quota of overs in reaching a paltry 132 for 3. Gavaskar had decided there was no way in which they could reach such a target and batted through the full 60 overs to reach 36 not out! A great day to be a cricket commentator!

By far the best of the matches was at Leeds when Australia gave an early warning of serious intent by beating Pakistan by 73 runs. It was due largely to the effort of Ross Edwards, with a brilliant 80 not out, that Australia reached 278 for 7 which one felt had to be a winning score. Pakistan quickly showed their fighting qualities and after early reverses Majid and Asif Iqbal, matching each other with their audacity of stroke play, had rallied the side to 172 for 4 with 20 overs still to go. Not for the first time Australia had a man equal to the occasion and Lillee returning to the attack, broke through, cleaned up the later order batsmen and returned the fine figures of 5 for 34. The much publicised Thomson on his first appearance in England completely lost his rhythm and bowled only eight overs which included 12 no balls. Headingley had packed in 22,000 people that day and provided the glorious weather continued, the success of the Prudential Cup was assured.

In fact the sun continued to beat down when the second series of games began four days later. England moved on to Nottingham to meet their most serious group rivals, New Zealand and it was solely due to the brilliance of Keith Fletcher that they retained their 100 per cent record and made certain of a semi-final place. Fletcher, free of inhibitions and at his very best completely dominated the England innings after Amiss and Jameson had gone cheaply. He was run out off the last ball of the innings with his score on 131 and England's total 266. The early loss of Turner acted as a bitter blow to New Zealand after which Greig taking 4 for 45 made sure that they never got back into the game. India played East Africa at Leeds and quickly showed the disparity between the sides collecting their first points with an easy 10 wickets victory. In direct contrast to the gate four days earlier only 720 people paid to watch this one-sided affair.

Two hundred miles further south at Kennington Oval the other underdogs Sri Lanka were meeting the might of Australia and what a different story this turned out to be. To all intents and purposes the game was going along in the expected fashion with Turner, McCosker, Greg Chappell and Walters helping themselves to runs in reaching 328 for 5. The surprise of the summer was upon us when Sri Lanka faced the Australians' speed attack. With a series of well executed hooks and cuts the Sri Lankans rattled the score along and for a change the Australians found themselves on the receiving end. Thomson, still without a wicket in England, hospitalised two batsmen but it had no effect on those that followed who showed great courage, refused to be intimidated and continued to get right in line and carried on playing shots. In fact they did it to such great effect that when time had run out for them, their score had reached a wonderful 276 for 4, only 52 runs adrift. The Australian pace attack of Lillee, Thomson and Walker could only show combined bowling figures of 1 for 108. Australia collected the points but Sri Lanka a host of new admirers.

Back at Birmingham there was an absolute cup thriller played between Pakistan and West Indies. Pakistan began by mastering the all-seam West Indies attack. Majid (60), Zaheer (31), Mushtaq (55) and Wasim Raja (58) gave full reign to their flowing stroke play and a final score of 266 for 7 left them full of confidence. When Sarfraz began to cut his way through the West Indians' batting with only Lloyd (53) offering any sort of resistance the favourites had crashed to 166 for 8 – 101 runs wanted and only Andy Roberts to bat! Holder, joining the ever dependable Murray, took the score to 203 before giving Sarfraz his fourth wicket. Thus a further 64 were wanted by the last pair in 14 overs. It never seemed possible but gradually and despite frequent bowling changes Murray and Roberts with a great sense of discipline pushed the score nearer and nearer and to the great jubilation of their supporters and the utter amazement of the Pakistanis they scampered the winning run from the fourth ball of the last over.

The third series played on 14th June included two vital games, vital for different reasons. With England already through to the semi-final the clash between India and New Zealand would decide who joined them. In group B both West Indies and Australia were unbeaten and therefore certain to go forward. Their meeting at the Oval would not affect that issue but this was the match that the whole cricketing world looked forward to with eager anticipation. Every seat had been sold weeks in advance. The streets in Brixton and Earls Court must have been deserted as Lloyd won the toss and with sufficient cloud cover around to help his new ball bowlers, put Australia in. Roberts, Julien and Boyce in turn responded to the call and Australia were tottering at 61 for 5 when Marsh joined Edwards. They took the score to 160 before Edwards was bowled by occasional bowler Richards and Marsh, with no support at all from the tail, was left high and dry with 52 not out as Australia were dismissed for 192.

Now was to come the moment of truth for West Indies. Their first confrontation with Lillee and Thomson, the outcome of which might have an important bearing on their clashes over the next 12 months. As it happened it was little Roy Fredericks who decided to get in the first psychological blows and with a series of hooks and cuts threw Lillee, in particular, completely off balance. His first wicket partnership with Kallicharan bordered on the sensational and left the huge West Indian following delirious with excitement. Between them they plundered the Australian attack to such an extent that the diminutive Kallicharan personally improved his score by 35 off 10 successive balls from Lillee. When they were dismissed in fairly rapid succession only 34 runs were wanted with seven wickets in hand and Richards and Kanhai made these with ease and with 14 overs to spare. The Australians had been outplayed in every department of the game. There was however a strong possibility that these two fine sides may yet contest the Lords final and one had the feeling that the Australians would not be such easy meat the next time round.

Up at Old Trafford a ding-dong struggle took place between India and New Zealand on a good batting pitch. Thanks to a spirited 70 by Abid Ali, India with a final score of 230 had set New Zealand a testing target. It was yet again only the brilliance, coupled with the calmness, of Glenn Turner that made a victory for New Zealand possible. Watching his colleagues struggling at the other end as wickets fell at regular intervals, he made his way to a superb undefeated 114 before allowing his No. 8 batsman, Dayle Hadlee, the privilege of hitting the winning run with just 13 balls left. The two other games went as expected with England humiliating East Africa at Birmingham and across at Trent Bridge Pakistan proving much too strong for Sri Lanka. The League matches were completed and the tables were as follows.

Group A			Group B		
England	12 points		West Indies	12 points	
New Zealand	8	,,	Australia	8	,,
India	4	,,	Pakistan	4	,,
East Africa	0	,,	Sri Lanka	0	,,

The semi-finals embraced the leaders of group A (England) against the runners-up in group B (Australia) to be played at Headingley whilst at the Oval West Indies met New Zealand to decide who would go through to Lords.

For some inconceivable reason the Headingley groundsman decided that this all-important tie would be played on the same pitch used for Australia versus Pakistan 10 days earlier. The unusually hot spell of weather had necessitated watering it and the strip was unrecognisable as the one that produced 483 runs the previous game. Shrewd assessment of the situation by Ian Chappell resulted in the new ball being handed to Gary Gilmour, a dangerous swing bowler under these conditions, in preference to Thomson as Amiss and Wood opened for England. Quick to seize his opportunity Gilmour proceeded to exploit conditions to the full in a wonderful exhibition of new-ball bowling which drew exclamations of approval from the huge Headingley crowd. At the same time he was aided and abetted by the early England batsmen who mistakenly tried to counter the late swing and movement of the pitch by remaining on the back foot. They paid the penalty in full with four of them going LBW plus Wood yorked and Greig taken by wicketkeeper Marsh. Gilmour returned the staggering figures of 12-6-14-6, Denness and Arnold were the only batsmen to reach double figures and England, in the short space of 36 overs, were dismissed for 93.

With the Australians similarly suspicious about the quality of the pitch the drama was not yet over. England's attack of Snow, Arnold and particularly Old hit back in great style and had Australia reeling at 39 for 6. With the shaky Walters, the lone survivor, and later batsmen of doubtful quality to come, it would not need a miracle for England to bring off a remarkable victory. Gary Gilmour must have felt it really was his day as he joined Walters and at once cracked two glorious off drives to the fence. There was no holding him and with no margin of error allowable to the England bowlers, he quickly put the issue beyond doubt. An unbroken partnership of 55 with Walters saw his side home in 28 overs and a game which had brought a capacity crowd to Leeds had been completed in 65 overs. Both captains strongly criticised the pitch, and rightly so, and nobody could successfully defend the action of the groundsman for a fixture as important as this one.

At Kennington Oval, Clive Lloyd continued his policy of insertion when he won the toss and New Zealand found runs hard to come by in face of the keen, lively and accurate West

Indies attack. A pretty grim struggle ensued, Turner as ever surviving the early onslaught but never able to break loose. The one challenging innings came most appropriately from the Surrey-based New Zealander, Geoff Howarth. A young player of immense talent, if at times lacking in concentration, he reached an excellent half century before falling to Roberts. The pressure of this keen bowling attack was altogether too much for the rest of New Zealand's batting and after being 92 for 1 at lunch, they quickly subsided to an all out score of 158. There was early encouragement for them when Hadlee snapped up the wicket of Fredericks but Greenidge and Kallicharan in a rapid partnership of 125 put the issue beyond doubt. The left-hander hooked, drove and cut with devastating effect and when he finally departed for 72 only another 17 runs were required. West Indies by a comfortable margin of five wickets were through to the final against Australia at Lords which promised to be one of the great cricket occasions of our time.

There had scarcely been a cloud in the sky over the preceeding two weeks and Saturday, June 21st, proved to be no exception. The date in my diary 'the longest day' could not have been better described with the two finest sides in the world locked in highly entertaining conflict from 11 a.m. until 8.45 p.m. watched by 26,000 people who paid £66,950. Where else in the sporting world could you see such a spectacle lasting the best part of ten hours for an average cost per head of less than £2.60? It was dear old Alec Skelding who described the white-coated officials as the 'unconsidered umpires'. Umpires usually only hit the headlines when they are under criticism and earn very few bouquets when they do a good job. There can be no doubt that Tom Spencer and Harold Bird had an outstanding day in this Prudential Cup Final and one cannot praise them too highly. Umpires lose the toss every day and six hours is normally sufficient to test the concentration of the most zealous. That they survived this long gruelling day and its electric atmosphere and gave numerous decisions without upsetting a single person was an outstanding performance.

The first news was that Ian Chappell had taken a leaf out of Clive Lloyd's book and on winning the toss had put West Indies in to bat and with only 12 runs on the board, Australia struck the first blow. Fredericks could consider himself desperately unlucky. He played a wonderful hook shot off a Lillee bouncer and as the ball disappeared for six over long leg, he had the misfortune to overbalance and break his wicket. There was to be no Oval repeat from Kallicharan, faced now with a much more accurate Lillee and the Headingley hero Gilmour who again looked the pick of the Australian bowlers.

Kallicharan soon fell to a catch by Marsh, as did Greenidge who was never able to put his game together. West Indies were struggling at 50 for 3 when Lloyd joined Kanhai. The West Indian captain had virtually held a watching brief as his side had steam-rollered their way to the final and had only taken guard on two occasions but Lords has always been a happy hunting ground for big Clive and one felt again that this could be his day. He quickly announced himself with a massive hook for six off Lillee and turning his attention to Max Walker he produced a series of shots of phenomenal power which had his supporters on their feet clamouring for more. He did not let them down and raced to a glorious century in just about even time after receiving only 82 balls. Some years previously the great Kanhai could not have sat back without coming into the act himself. Quite out of character he adopted the role of anchor man and proceeded to play an innings of inestimable value to his side. Content to take a single and leave the principal action to the man who had replaced him as captain, he would periodically produce a classic square drive just to let this huge crowd know he was still around. Between them, Lloyd (102) and Kanhai (55) had again blunted the attack and left the way open for Boyce and Julian to add more exciting runs to complete the 60 overs. Out of West Indies' score of 291 for 8 Gary Gilmour had once again done a fine job as his bowling figures of 5 for 48 clearly showed.

A target of five runs per over represented a highly improbable but not necessarily impossible task and despite losing the early wicket of McCosker, Australia made a good start. Ian Chappell in particular was in good form and with solid support coming from Alan Turner it seemed we could have a real thriller on our hands. Suddenly and quite unaccountably within a short space of time, Turner, Ian Chappell and his brother Greg had run themselves out. At this sort of level one seldom sees an Australian, let alone, three senior ones, make elementary errors in the judgement of a run but limited-over cricket calls for all kinds of qualities, not least of which is mathematical prowess.

Australia had to keep up to somewhere near the required run rate otherwise too much pressure would be put on the later batsmen and the thought that they might not be pushing the score along quite fast enough was the root cause of these dismissals.

For all that, they could still turn to a very handy quartet in Walters, Marsh, Edwards and Gilmour. Walters, with every shot in the book at his disposal, must surely come good at some time in England. Marsh with the ability to alter the course of any game in a short space of time, Edwards in excellent form and Gilmour a lively and dangerous hitter. It was not to be, for though Walters and Edwards played well enough the turning point came in a burst from Keith Boyce who took three of those four wickets in a good accurate spell. With Max Walker, would you believe, run out it was surely the end for Australia, the score standing at 233 for 9 as Lillee joined his pace bowling colleague Thomson. We all knew, at least we thought we knew, that it was all over – there was no way in which these two could score 59 to win, but an Australian with his back to the wall does not yield easily and in the last half hour Lillee and Thomson gave a further example of the greatness of our summer game. A combination of fine drives and a few narrow escapes kept the scoreboard officials busy and between them the last pair had added 41 runs and remarkably had given their side the chance of pulling off a sensational win. Now only 18 more runs were wanted and eight balls were left when for the fifth time in the innings two Australians embarked on an impossible run. The speed and agility of the West Indians in the field was too much for them, Thomson was run out for 21, the crowd streamed out on to the field and West Indies had won a great match by the narrow margin of 17 runs.

Clive Lloyd, quite rightly named as man of the match, hoisted the Prudential Trophy high above his head and the West Indians were finally acknowledged as the kings of the one-day game.

So ended the greatest experiment in our cricket history though it achieved its greatness because it was supremely successful. It was successful because of the efficient organisation, the performances of the players themselves and not least, perfect English summer weather.

Turning to the financial aspect the gross revenue from sponsorship and gate receipts was £300,000 out of which the winners received £4000, the runners-up £2000 and the losing semi-finalists £1000 each. The net profit after all expenses had been deducted was split as follows:

10 per cent to the U.K. as hosts.

7½ per cent to the other seven participating countries.

37 per cent to the International Cricket Conference to distribute at their discretion, making sure that a percentage would be held in reserve for the next International World Cup.

Enthusiasm for this first ever World Cup had swept the country and naturally everyone was debating when and where it could all happen again. The matter came up for further discussion when the I.C.C. met in London towards the end of June and representatives were invited to submit their thoughts and ideas.

Fairly obviously England would be the most favourable of all venues, equipped with sufficient good grounds, very accessible and of course the only country able to play through until 8 p.m. on a June evening. The chief problem could be the unreliability of our climate and a very full fixture list over the next few years. A wet June could easily cause chaos and make the competition as big a flop as it had been a success in 1975. Australia are due in England for a full tour in 1977 followed by the visits of Pakistan and New Zealand in 1978. India are earmarked to have 1979 to themselves and this would seem the first available date, and would bring us in line with soccer with a four-year gap between competitions.

As I see it the only other country with rival claims would be India who have already said they would be keen to act as hosts. Very much in their favour is the weather and they certainly have the grounds with little doubt that they would be packed to capacity. Geographically it is ideal and the one criticism is the shortage of daylight hours compared to the U.K. It is, on the other hand, a possibility that play could commence $1-1\frac{1}{2}$ hours earlier than in England and with weather prospects certainly guaranteed, the odd matches that could not be completed in a single day could overspill without too much worry. Still I believe the I.C.C. will risk our weather and will contemplate the second World Cup taking place in England in 1979. In common with all I am sure it will be well worth waiting for.

The Fenner Trophy,
The Warwick Pool
and Trobriand Cricket

The Scarborough Festival has, for well over 50 years, been set aside as the grande finale of our cricket season. Every cricketer worth his salt has journeyed North to enjoy 10 days by the sea and play cricket in the most relaxed atmosphere one could imagine. After a hard competitive season there was no longer any pressure, either on or off the field, so much so in fact, that often one was in need of a holiday once the Festival ended. It was rare indeed that a batsman ever made a nought and any player arriving a few runs short of a thousand for the season or needing a wicket or two to reach a hundred seldom returned with his mission unfulfilled. Nightly parties would go on into the early hours of the morning and many a batsman has had the greatest difficulty in keeping his balance as he took guard! I well recall watching one of our most eminent post-war cricketers aiming three unsuccessful blows with his bat at an offending piece of turf before he finally made contact. The festival for years was supported in great strength by the Yorkshire holiday makers, earmarked in their diaries as soon as the dates were announced. In many ways it was remarkable that Yorkshire folk entered into the spirit of this light-hearted carefree approach to a game so opposed to the dour Roses battles at Bramall Lane. Still enjoy it they did and they kept coming back in their thousands.

My first invitation to Scarborough came in 1948, the year of Sir Donald Bradman's all conquering Australians, and I arrived there with something of a chip on my shoulder, having a few days earlier been omitted from the M.C.C. touring party for South Africa. For a couple of seasons I had been accustomed to living with our own detestable brand of discrimination in relation to the amateur and professional but did not

75

believe it would be in evidence at Scarborough. As one
of three professionals representing Mr. H.D.G. Leveson-
Gower's XI, I was horrified to discover that lunch for the
teams laid out in a nearby marquee did not include the paid
ranks, who instead remained in the pavilion at a bare wooden
table with a ham salad that would not have made a good
hors-d'oeuvre. I made sure that I collected my match fees
before telling Mr. H.D.G. what he could do in future years
with his Festival. Not surprisingly I never returned. Happily
those days are well behind us and all cricketers have subsequently relished their visits to the Festival.

It was noticeable that in common with County cricket,
attendances in the late 60's, even at Scarborough, had begun
to dwindle quite alarmingly and no game was more seriously
affected than the traditional opener between M.C.C. and
Yorkshire. Very often this game clashed with a number of
County fixtures still in progress and it did not help that the
M.C.C. side was often far from representative of our top
players. So it was that J.H. Fenner, the Hull Power Trans-
mission Company came to the rescue to sponsor a new three-
day, limited-over knock-out competition. Fenner had supported Yorkshire cricket for many years in a variety of ways
in addition to employing two great Yorkshire stalwarts in Sir
Leonard Hutton and more recently Willie Watson in their
Johannesburg office. The host County, Yorkshire, were to be
joined each year by three invited counties and those selected
to take part in the first Fenner trophy competition with £1000
offered in prize money, were Lancashire, Kent and Nottinghamshire. The first two had just previously met in the Gillette
Cup Final and I can only presume that Nottinghamshire were
there with the promise that Gary Sobers would boost the
gate. The games of 50 overs each were an immediate success,
with the attendance over the three days in excess of 30,000.
Kent and Lancashire met in the final and the hop country
extracted some revenge for their defeat at Lords and became
the first side to hold the Fenner Trophy.

For six years now the competition has grown in strength
and continues to fill the North Marine ground. Yorkshire
naturally have continued to be host and their visitors have
now included Hampshire, Sussex, Worcestershire, Surrey,

Gloucestershire, and Warwickshire as well as the three original contenders. The Trophy has now been won twice by Kent, Hampshire and Yorkshire. The sides yet to be invited are Derbyshire, Glamorgan, Essex, Somerset, Middlesex, Northants and Leicestershire. It seems there is still plenty of entertaining cricket due to come the way of the Scarborough holiday makers.

The leading exponents of one-day cricket have again stolen the honours. Brian Luckhurst has made two of the six hundreds scored to date. Chris Old cracked a brilliant 106 in just 75 minutes and Richard Gilliat an equally devastating 124. I rather imagine that the day they all remember was the 1975 Final. To the delight of 14,000 spectators, local hero Geoffrey Boycott gave them a flawless exhibition of top-class stroke play in making 116 out of Yorkshire's 240 for 6 (50 overs). If this was to be matched by anyone else it just had to be the great Barry Richards. Not only did he do just that as Hampshire made 243 for 3 but he was still there at the death with an undefeated hundred and Hampshire still had more than four overs to spare.

Bowling successes, as one has come to expect, occur much less frequently with just three players with five wickets in an innings to their name. Tony Nicholson tops the bill closely followed by those fine spinners, Derek Underwood and Jack Simmons.

Long may the Fenner Trophy remain in our cricket calendar.

Records
    Highest Total – 290 for 8 Hampshire v Gloucestershire, 1975.
    Lowest Total – 59 Warwickshire v Yorkshire, 1974.
    Highest individual score – 141 n.o. B. Luckhurst (Kent), 1973.
    Best bowling – 5 for 23 A.G. Nicholson (Yorkshire), 1974.

The Warwick Pool Under 25 County Cricket Competition

If many people were far from being convinced that one-day

or limited-over cricket was here to stay, then Mr. Cyril Goodway, the vibrant chairman of Warwickshire County Cricket Club, was not one of them. It became apparent to him that we should shortly reach a situation where young inexperienced members of a County playing staff would be thrown in at the deep end and with little or no idea of the tactics required in limited-over cricket. It seemed obvious to him that some similar form of competitive afternoon cricket should be used as a training ground prior to their promotion to the more publicised competitions. In fact a junior competition played amongst the first-class Counties would be the ideal answer though there were at least three very solid stumbling blocks.

With an already congested fixture list, there was no way in which a full programme could be achieved. Secondly, there might well be a serious disruption of County Second XI cricket and thirdly the cost of promoting and running such an exclusive competition was completely beyond the bounds of possibility. Still problems are there to be overcome and Cyril Goodway is the last man to be put off by inconveniences such as these. With the co-operation of four County secretaries and the very able assistance of Alan Oakman, a committee was formed to see what could be done. They quickly overcame problem number one by dividing the counties into four zones, ie North, South, Midlands and West, which consequently reduced the number of fixtures and virtually cut out the need for overnight expenses. The matches in the zones were to be played on a league basis with the winners of each section going forward to the semi-final ties. The counties co-operated to the full, though after the first season Northants decided to withdraw, feeling that the money expended could be better spent on Second XI cricket. In an effort to ease the financial outlay, Mr. Goodway approached his own Warwickshire Supporters Association, that highly efficient body who for years had worked wonders in helping to finance the County. They agreed to act as sponsors to provide a sum of £500 to the winning County, £250 to the losing finalists and £125 each to the other two semi-finalists; these sums to be paid directly to the County Clubs concerned, for them to distribute in such a way as they felt appropriate.

There has of necessity been several changes to the rules over the last five years, not the least important of which has been a further increase in sponsorship money. The Supporters Association now pay a sum of £200 to each County completing their fixtures but for this to be possible they have reduced the prize money to the winners to £200, £100 and £50 respectively.

The competition is restricted to uncapped players under 25 years of age on the 1st April in the relevant year who are identified with first-class clubs. Players who are awarded a County or possibly a Country Cap during the season are eligible to continue to play until the end of the season. The organisers would like, if possible, that the captains of the teams should also be under 25 but offer no reasonable objection if a county feels strongly that the team should be led by its Coach, though they would be particularly concerned if the County slipped in a seasoned capped player with a view to making a positive contribution towards the winning of matches.

Significantly Middlesex won the competition in 1972, 1973, 1974 and lost in the final in 1975. Under the expertise of Don Bennett, the County has produced a crop of really fine young players and the value of this competition is underlined by the fact that several of them have successfully made the transition to the seniors; Graham Barlow, Mike Gatting, Nigel Ross, Ian Gould and even the redoubtable Wayne Daniel have all benefitted from this early experience. Middlesex are certain to be a force to be reckoned with over the next few years in every form of cricket. Similarly the side that overcame them in 1975, namely Leicestershire, have few worries about their future. Gower and Briers, Clift and Humphreys have in turn been the stars of their Under-25 side and when the day dawns when Illingworth, Higgs and company finally hang up their boots, this competition will have played a vital role in helping to provide suitable replacements.

At the time of writing there is some doubt as to whether the Warwick Pool will be able to maintain their sponsorship. Their vast profits over the years have dwindled considerably and they have unfortunately reached a stage when they must seriously consider if they are still able to continue their generous sponsorship. It would be a sad day if this competition were to lapse into obscurity and finally wind up.

Trobriand Cricket

The Trobriand islands lie among the coral-strewn seas to the east of Papua, New Guinea. An unlikely setting you might think for one-day cricket, and the islanders unlikely participants. Reports of their games are hardly likely to reach the international press nor have record books been published on the outcome of these contests. There is far more to their game than winning or losing or mundane matters such as winning bonuses or 'Man of the Match' awards, all of which pale into insignificance as these games unfold. The players are experts in their own right and can point to 80 years experience in one-day cricket.

No real need to dwell on the point that it was a Britisher and a missionary, the Rev. M.K. Gilmour, who introduced the game of cricket just before the turn of the century. Their present cricket fields were once the arenas for ritual wars between the villages. Vicious and bloody battles took place there and if no spear has been thrown in anger since the Rev. M.K. arrived with his Bible and his Wisden, there is no mistaking the presence in their cricket of their ancient art of warfare.

The Trobrianders are not beset with financial problems, have no worries about inflation and no cause to look for sponsorship. A machete is the sole tool of the goundsmen, of whom there is no shortage of volunteers. Their entire equipment for the game comprises simply wickets, bats and balls, and all are hand-made prior to the contest. The axe, which a hundred years ago was used for sharpening a spear is now used to deftly shape the ball cut out of hardwood. Even John Snow would be hard pressed to convince anyone that this ball would lose its original shape and if it might allow movement off the pitch, Denis Lillee would find swing in the air an impossibility. Similarly the craftsmen go to work to carve out the one-piece bats – the finished product being something akin to the curved and rounded bats used here in the last century. Without television there is no call for them to be plastered with modern advertising gimmicks. It seems in fact, that the islanders have not progressed with the times but rather gone back to the medieval state and who can argue that in many ways it is no bad idea. Pads and gloves are discounted but it is interesting to note that in place of our abdominal protector they favour a highly decorative pubic cover though observing the size of it, one can only conclude it is an integral part of the dress rather than a vital piece of protection.

The Trobrianders discard any thought of net practice but rather spend the day prior to the match in deadly serious rehearsal perfecting the ritual dances and chants which inevitably follow a good catch in the field. Fixing the weather remains the final problem and the rain magician is considered of even greater importance than the umpires and he remains the one paid member present. The islanders would never consider an activity such as this without his valued assistance. Thus the great day arrives and hardly has the sun broken through before the visiting team surrounded by supporters are threading and dancing their way through the outer perimeter in full voice. There is nothing in their laws to stipulate how many should play in each side provided there are an equal number in both teams. A good average is about 60 per side and as it is to be a two innings game, it is possible for 240 wickets to fall in the day's play. How accurate the scoring is likely to be is anyone's guess but can only be as accurate as the scorer himself, armed with machete and coconut frond. With the best part of 60 fielders, no specialist batsmen or bowlers (every player is deemed to be an all-rounder) and an uneven pitch, the dice is heavily loaded in the bowlers' favour. The term 'bowler' is a gracious one as not a single Trobriand action would pass the scrutiny of a Fagg or a Bird. The ball, in fact, is propelled as a spear would have been a century earlier; wickets therefore tumble in rapid succession and they must if the game is to be completed before nightfall. For all that, the runs that are scored accumulate at a ferocious pace, particularly as the forward defensive push has never reached these distant islands and the players still believe the bat is there to hit the ball with.

This all-action cricket invariably carries on till dusk, by which time the players who have never stopped running, dancing and chanting throughout the long day. are usually to be seen totally exhausted as the sun finally disappears from the sky. Despite the intense rivalry between the villagers, and the intimidation incorporated into the songs and dances, the final result is usually of little importance. It would be considered the greatest insult of all if the visiting side should ever happen to win.

A typical cricket match was once filmed and shown by the B.B.C. in an 'Horizon' programme in December 1975. The islanders were keen on the portrayal of their cricket as they believe there is a great tourist possibility in these, yet un-spoiled islands, and they look to their ancient game as a further attraction.

Perhaps one day we may see an England side breaking their journey to challenge the locals at one-day cricket. Even if it opens up the possibility of Derek Underwood taking 80 wickets in a day's play, I rather fancy that played under Trobriand rules my money would be firmly on the home side.

A Great One-day Match,
Memorable One-day Innings
and Best Ever One-day Eleven

For as long as I watch one-day cricket I cannot seriously believe I shall see a more dramatic day's cricket than the Gillette Cup semi-final played at Old Trafford between Lancashire and Gloucestershire on 28 July 1971. Apart from an hour's delay through rain at lunchtime continuous play extended from 11 a.m. to 8.50 p.m. in front of a crowd officially estimated at 23,520 who paid receipts of £9,738. I am sure the latter figure is a correct one but remain unconvinced of the attendance figure which would never take into account the hundreds of 'free-loaders' coming in over the top.

The vast crowd was still streaming in and jockeying for position as Tony Brown won the toss for Gloucester and decided to bat on a perfect pitch of easy pace. Nobody was more anxious to do well than David Green, formerly of Lancashire, who in the company of Ron Nicholls weathered the early attack of Lever and Shuttleworth. An opening stand of 57 gave Gloucester the necessary base before Green was run out. Nicholls battled on for an admirable 50 but it was the mighty Procter who held the stage; a string of superb drives brought him nine 4's and a six in his 65 before Farouk Engineer took a brilliant catch to dismiss him. The score was then 150 for 3 and Gloucester were ahead on points. Not for the first time Lancashire turned to the burly Jack Simmons to provide an answer. His immaculate off spin brought his side back into the game, bowling his 12 overs for only 25 runs and a couple of wickets. At 210 for 6 the odds now favoured Lancashire and despite an aggressive 29 not out from Mike Bissex, a final score of 229 left me feeling that the visitors were 30 or 40 runs short and a score of 230 was well within Lancashire's compass on a pitch unaffected by the rain and offering no help to the bowlers.

83

As is their wont Lancashire looked for a solid start from David Lloyd and Barry Wood and this they duly supplied. Although the first 50 had taken 17 overs and eleven runs later Lloyd fell to Tony Brown, Harry Pilling and Barry Wood saw them safely into three figures and it seemed the game was theirs for the taking. John Mortimore had different ideas. After the departure of Wood and Pilling, the Gloucester off spinner, in a fine accurate spell, clean bowled Clive Lloyd and induced Farouk Engineer to hit his wicket. With Davey accounting for Sullivan, Lancashire had slumped to 163 for 6 and the game again was wide open. This enormous and vibrant crowd who previously had been cherishing and cheering every run went quiet. The clock had crept past the 7.30 p.m. mark and the light was gradually worsening, umpires Bird and Jepson consulted and play went on. The new batsmen in charge were 'Skipper' Bond and Jack Simmons and they badly needed to right the ship. With typical Lancastrian common sense and no trace of panic they went about their task skilfully and professionally and the colour gradually began to come back into the faces of the Lancashire supporters. These two added 40 runs, defying all the bowling changes made by Tony Brown, until Mortimore broke through again and bowled Simmons to make it 203 for 7. Twenty-seven were wanted, three wickets in hand and six overs left. By this time it seemed impossible that the game could be finished that day. It was now very, very dark, the pavilion light casting shadows on the enclosure and in the background Old Trafford station had been ablaze with lights for some time. The umpires only needed a nod from Jack Bond for the play to be suspended when down the pavilion steps appeared David Hughes unnoticed for more than one reason. The focus was on Bond. Would he now decide to call it a day? He goes on record as saying that his first thought was to ensure that this noisy excitable crowd would not be deprived of a finish that day. It would be a terrible anticlimax to come back the following day and complete the final 20 minutes or so in front of 10 men and a dog. Jack Bond is an extremely honest man and I believe his thinking would be along those lines. Perhaps it was also supported by the fact that Gloucester had already been in the field for well over three hours and the strain was beginning to tell. Of the six overs left Procter and Davey could bowl four of them and after a night's rest may well be a different proposition in the morning. Any lingering doubts he had were dispelled by the confidence of David Hughes who maintains that he purposely sat in a dark corner of the dressing room 'to become accustomed to the light'! His reply to Bond's instructions to look for the singles was 'if I can see them, skipper, I think I can hit them'.

In view of what followed it must have been the understatement of the year. Most people will forget that Hughes came within a whisker of being bowled first ball by John Mortimore and batted through a fine over from Davey who was extremely difficult to pick up at all. In this light their only chance was to attack the slow off spin of John Mortimore and what followed must go down as one of the most remarkable overs of all time. The unfortunate Mortimore was hammered for 24 runs in his next over in a wonderful exhibition of shrewd and skilful hitting by David Hughes. There was no wild slogging or hitting across the line and it seemed it was almost premeditated execution. By dint of excellent footwork the first ball was hit over extra cover safely for four and the second deposited in the crowd at long on for a mighty straight six. The crowd was going wild, up and down in their seats as Hughes, running like a hare put the third ball through the off side for two and the fourth wide of mid on for two more. The cover drive off the fifth ball for another four was the shot of the match and nobody could have bettered it. To crown it all the last ball was hit high and handsomely for six over mid on and unbelievably the scores were level. Appropriately it was left to Bond to nudge Procter wide of gully for a single and the crowd errupted. The entire playing area was invaded, Lancashire had won a famous victory with David Hughes so rightly adjudged Man of the Match. The same people who had been queuing for a seat at 8 o'clock that morning were rushing to get the last bus home from the ground after 10 o'clock that night.

Jack Bond asserts that it took weeks to get over it, and no doubt David Hughes is still accepting drinks as a result of his memorable achievement!

In acclaiming Lancashire's great day one cannot help but

sympathise with Gloucester and John Mortimore, in particular. I can think of no reason for John to reproach himself or believe that he was responsible for his side's defeat. The fatal over did not include a solitary bad ball, although one could possibly argue that he might have pushed the ball through quickly on a fuller length around the leg stump. This has never been John Mortimore's method. Praise be that he always goes down in my book as an attacking bowler and did he not previously account for Lloyd, Engineer and Simmons in this manner? For three minutes in that match he was unlucky to run across a man totally inspired who produced half a dozen shots worthy of being ranked with the greatest of our time and when that happens, no matter who the bowler is, there is precious little that anyone can do about it.

One of the least publicised facts about this game and one which I am sure in retrospect had a profound bearing on the result concerned the final period of play. The Gloucester side in fact must have achieved some kind of record with an unbroken spell of four hours in the field. There would be a public outcry if any side were asked to field from start of play at 11.30 a.m. right the way through until the tea interval which, of course, is the equivalent of Gloucester's marathon effort in the field. A 20-minute break in that final period would have allowed them vital breathing space, a chance coolly to reassess the situation and break the Lancashire concentration, all of which must have been very much in their favour.

If the players unanimously agreed that it was some time before they recovered from their efforts, the same may also be said of the T.V. commentary team. For some time our producer in charge of B.B.C.1 cricket, David Kenning, had the happy knack of selecting the best of the one-day matches but on this occasion he was, for once, thwarted by the weather. Believing that the thrills and excitement of the semi-final would come from the other game between two evenly-matched sides, Kent and Warwickshire, he took himself off to Canterbury along with Peter West and Richie Benaud and posted me North to complement the main coverage from Old Trafford. Only as an afterthought did he book Tony Lewis to help me out and make his television debut as a commentator. The inevitable of course happened – Old Trafford was bathed in sunshine most of the day, and Canterbury was awash with overnight rain. A little after 10 a.m. Tony and I took up our position in the commentary box and apart from a short break, when a shower held up play, recorded just about every ball bowled until we finally descended the scaffolding shortly after 9 p.m. For obvious reasons we sat cross-legged over the last three hours! Soon after 8 p.m. we had a call from the Controller of B.B.C.1, Paul Fox, asking if there was any chance of the game still being in progress at 8.50 p.m. Peering through the gloom, I replied that there was no chance unless the game was transferred over the road to the floodlights at the other Old Trafford. As everyone knows play did go on and at 8.50 p.m. I received a message that on a 10-second count down, the game would be taken live into the National News. Thus cricket history was made and no one-day game that I have ever witnessed was more deserving of the immense publicity that surrounded it.

Memorable One-Day Innings

It is, I am sure, true to say that there are more lasting memories connected with the game of cricket than any other sport. Spending an hour at Lords in the company of G.O. Allen and E.W. Swanton must inevitably include accounts of some stirring events over the past 40 or 50 years. This august company is not exceptional in its nostalgia and one can expect to listen to similar memories in the most humble of Cricket Club premises.

In its own way one-day cricket, despite being in its comparative infancy, has already made its mark in this respect and already I, for one, have vivid recollections of some of the great individual performances which I shall treasure for many a long day.

Difficult as the problem is I have selected seven of the best innings I can recall and have even had the temerity to place them in my own order of merit which obviously is open to a fair amount of criticism. Having tried to assess such performances in terms of batting conditions, the sense of occasion, the state of the game and the strength or weakness of the opposition, my final ratings are as follows:

1   G. Boycott   Yorks. v Surrey (Gillette Cup Final, 1965) 146

2   B. Davison   Leics. v Warks. (B. & H. Coventry, 1972) 158*

3   C. Lloyd   Lancs. v Warks. (Gillette Cup Final, 1972) 126

4   B. Richards   Hants. v Yorks (J.P.L., Hull, 1970) 155*

5   G. Greenidge   Hants. v Glamorgan (Gillette, Soton, 1975) 177

6   Sadiq Mohammad   Glouc. v Somerset (J.P.L., Bristol) 1975) 131

7   V. Richards   Somerset v Gloucs. (J.P.L., Bristol, 1975) 126*

Geoffrey Boycott

The first surprising feature of the 1965 Gillette Cup Final was that it took place at all, as torrential rain lashed Lords for the whole of the preceding day and was still coming down well into the night.

Tremendous work by the ground staff disposed of the lakes in the outfield and play was possible by noon. Even so, with the whole ground still something of a soggy mess, giving no run to the ball whatsoever, it was generally agreed that 200 runs would represent a winning total and an individual 50 would be worth many a century under normal conditions. Since the war there has been intense rivalry between Yorkshire and Surrey with nothing asked for and certainly nothing given and as Geoff Boycott took guard at 12 o'clock he knew he had not only to overcome the conditions, but in Arnold and Pocock with pace and spin, he was faced with two of the brightest young prospects in English cricket. It is really inconceivable to relate that by the time he was sipping his tea and munching his piece of Lords' fruit cake, his personal contribution to Yorkshire's 317 for 4 was an amazing score of 146. The impossibly slow outfield had yielded him 15 fours and three further perfectly timed shots had cleared the boundary ropes. He had taken apart this Surrey attack in the manner of a great player in peak form and he had done it with a succession of superbly timed, authentic text book shots. If I had some problem in finding the correct order of the innings that follow there has never been any doubt in my mind that taking everything into consideration this Boycott century must rank as the greatest of all and I shall be most surprised if I see it bettered.

Brian Davison

Over the years I had almost despaired of seeing Brian Davison produce one of the electrifying innings of which he was doubtless capable. So often has he let us down on television after we had greeted his arrival at the crease with great enthusiasm and attempts to whet the viewer's appetite. May 13th, 1972 was the day he made up for everything that had gone before, or since, in a Benson & Hedges zonal match against Warwickshire at Coventry. Leicestershire, who batted first, were given a useful start by Duddleston and Norman and by the time Tolchard was out, their score stood on 91 for 2 after 25 overs. Thus only 30 overs remained when Davison joined Norman and what followed was hardly believable. In 28 overs and taking 88 minutes Davison and Norman added 227 runs.

The final Leicestershire score was 327 for 4, Brian Davison 158 not out. The brutal statistics reveal 10 sixes and 11 fours in this sensational innings which, in all, lasted 92 minutes. But there was more to it than that. Naturally all the bowlers suffered but in particular the two internationals, David Brown and Lance Gibbs. Brown, who had the help of a very strong wind behind him, looked menacing as he had bowled his first spell of five overs at a cost of a few paltry singles. His final analysis of 11 overs, one for 72 tells its own story. Davison hammered him unmercifully with a succession of stinging drives and several glorious straight sixes, driven with a ferocity seldom seen back over the bowler's head into the teeth of a near gale force wind over an extremely long straight boundary. At the other end the cunning Gibbs using the wind to vary his pace and flight was only slightly less expensive and he had to contend with a short leg side boundary which offered no sort of task for the belligerent Rhodesian. It was certainly one occasion when my task as a match adjudicator was a great deal simpler than my former role as off spin bowler.

Clive Lloyd

Later in the same year Warwickshire were again on the receiving end when a memorable performance from Clive Lloyd enabled Lancashire to carry off the Gillette Cup after a great Lords' Final. Warwickshire, who batted first, had reached 234 for 9 in their 60 overs on a good pitch, the sort of total which invariably will see a cracking finish. Anything over 300 or a score of less than 200 can often result in the game falling flat. Even so Lancashire were really up against it with both openers gone after 10 overs and the score on 26 when Lloyd appeared on the scene.

Warwickshire fully aware that his early dismissal would be the critical factor for them, threw everything they had at the big West Indian with nobody doing better than Bob Willis in a lively accurate spell. With 25,000 people sitting spellbound and tension mounting, all the ingredients were there to test the temperament of any batsman. Lloyd refused to be panicked into any rash ill-judgment of shot and coolly took stock, quietly playing himself in, taking eight overs to score his first six runs. Having satisfied himself that all was well he first of all turned his attention to David Brown, drove him straight with tremendous power for four and hooked the next, shorter one, for a glorious six. The floodgates had opened and from then on there was nothing to contain him. He hit the ball with such power that the fielders were powerless to cut off the steady stream of boundaries. In all he made 126 off 42 overs with three sixes and 14 fours and when he was finally adjudged lbw to the persevering Willis, his side were left with only 16 runs to make. The whole of Lords rose to him as he reached the Pavilion and I well remember Richie Benaud sitting alongside me saying it was the greatest innings he had ever seen at Lords. Many people will surely agree.

Barry Richards

One does not normally associate the Hull ground in Yorkshire with record-breaking feats of batting and indeed it had to be a really great batsman such as Barry Richards to have succeeded where so many before him have failed. Just how he succeeded in a John Player League match for Hampshire against Yorkshire in 1970 is illustrated by the fact that on that

June 15 day batsmen took guard, the collective total of 14 of them was 115 runs with 18 as the best effort. Barry Richards alone scored 155 not out from 142 balls received and hit three sixes and 24 fours. Six years later this incredible performance by Richards still stands supreme as the highest individual score made in a John Player League match.

One had grown accustomed to reading of a Richards' century, but taking several factors into account this innings must rank as his best ever in one-day cricket. The pitch at Hull normally gives a fair amount of help to all bowlers and the Yorkshire attack that day included Old, Richard Hutton and the admirable Tony Nicholson. With Cope and Wilson supplying spin it was ideally balanced and Reed, Turner and Livingstone were happy to survive and watch with wonderment at the brilliance of the South African. They managed to scramble 46 runs between them whilst Richards went serenely on his way to 155. The brilliance of his innings became more apparent when Yorkshire batted and 'Butch' White clean-bowled Boycott (4), Padgett (5), Hampshire (2) and Lead-beater (1) and Yorkshire suffered the humiliation of defeat by 141 runs. They could reflect that if Barry Richards had stayed in Southampton it may well have been a close contest.

Gordon Greenidge
Early in July of 1975 Glamorgan went down to Basingstoke and beat Hampshire by 66 runs in the process of which they dismissed Gordon Greenidge for a duck. A week later they met again, the venue was Southampton and the competition the Gillette Cup (second round). If this three-day defeat rankled with Hampshire they were to extract merciless revenge in the one-day game which shattered record after record. Southampton in the middle of a hot dry summer is a batsman's dream but even the most partisan home supporter could never have envisaged his side amassing a score of 371 for 4 from just 60 overs. For some considerable time Gordon Greenidge played a secondary role to the brilliant Richards as the two of them began with an opening stand of 210. Richards with a pre-lunch century, departed with 129 at which stage Greenidge had reached 73. During the next 20 overs he personally added a further 104 runs and his final score of 177

remains the highest individual total in any one-day competition.

The Glamorgan bowlers were ravaged unmercifully with the West Indian producing a full range of unstoppable shots which included seven sixes and seventeen fours in an exhibition of power batting seldom seen on the ground before. Malcolm Nash, as good a new ball bowler as one will find in one-day cricket was hammered for 84 runs from his 12 overs, Cordle was similarly treated. Solenky and Ellis were almost in the accurate category conceding only 15 runs per over. A day and an innings to remember indeed and in the unlikely event of Greenidge's score being beaten I hope I shall be there to see and record it.

Vivian Richards
Sadiq Mohammad

The local derby fixture between Somerset and Gloucestershire in the John Player League was played in 1975 on the Imperial Ground in Bristol. In terms of Sunday afternoon enjoyment it is difficult to recall a better John Player Match. All the right ingredients were there. A glorious day, a perfect pitch, a fast outfield and a capacity crowd enjoying the local rivalry. By the time the last wicket had fallen 525 runs had been scored (a league record) and it was by only the small margin of 15 runs that Somerset collected their winning bonus. Play was dominated by centuries from two overseas cricketers, Vivian Richards of Somerset leading the way with an unbeaten 126 only to be matched after tea by Gloucester's Sadiq who made a brilliant 131.

One would be hard-pressed to say which was the better performance but if I had been in the unenviable position of choosing a single man of the match, I believe I would have come down in favour of Sadiq. The first session of play belonged to Richards, who interestingly enough was dropped by Sadiq with his score on nine. He proceeded to make a mockery of the short boundary and in a furious display of hitting he dropped the ball into the crowd on six occasions and for good measure added a further 13 boundaries. With a score of 270 staring him in the face and the words of his captain ringing in his ears that he already owed his team 117 runs Sadiq, in partnership with Stovold, began what seemed an impossible task. He too had his share of good fortune when dropped by Close in the first over but undismayed the two openers even exceeded Somerset's run rate with a partnership of 123 in just 18 overs. It was only after Sadiq had reached his hundred in even time that three wickets (and victory hopes with them) fell quickly. Gloucester sadly missed the injured Procter and Sadiq, try as he could, was never able to hit any sixes. Perfectly timed cover drives fairly flowed from his bat until he was finally brilliantly caught by substitute Slocombe for a superb 131.

I think people who sat in the sun and watched the game and those who followed it in front of a television screen may well recall it in years to come. Probably not because of the record number of runs scored on a Sunday afternoon but because of the two brilliant individual performances. Richards from Antigua lived for a while in the shadow of his countryman Andy Roberts but has steadily forced his way to the top whilst Sadiq, for so long described as the younger brother of Hanif and Mushtaq, may yet prove himself to be the best of the three.

It cannot pass without notice that of the seven batsmen mentioned above the only Englishman is Geoff Boycott, which seems to confirm once again how the overseas cricketers have dominated one-day cricket. Looking through a list of 36 overseas players who have appeared regularly in recent seasons, 20 of them can be classified as specialist batsmen but only half that number as front line bowlers and the remaining six as genuine all-rounders. Thus, by and large, the Counties have scoured the overseas market for batsmen rather than bowlers and this again has been reflected in one-day cricket. Home bowlers have more than held their own and many of the outstanding bowling performances in one-day cricket have come the way of the Englishmen. Unfortunately it is an impossible task to list in any sort of order some of the outstanding feats of the bowlers.

Limitations which beset bowlers in a game which appears tailor-made for batsmen make comparisons futile. At the same time it would be grossly unfair not to pay tribute to one or two achievements which have found their way into one-day statistics.

Taking pride of place must be the performance of Brian Langford in a John Player League match at Yeovil when Somerset entertained Essex, and he never took a single wicket. If one-day cricket is about containing batsmen rather than dismissing them Brian Langford's figures can never be surpassed. He achieved the ultimate in bowling his eight overs without giving away a solitary run. No one has come even close to such a feat and dare it be said that he was an off spin bowler!

Standing high above all others are the match figures of Essex' Keith Boyce and on the face of it they are truly remarkable: 8 for 26 in 7·4 overs against Lancashire in a John Player League match in 1971. Without in any way wishing to detract from Keith's great day at Old Trafford, one must say that conditions were farcical, Essex had made 216 for 4 when a thunderstorm flooded Old Trafford. Under normal circumstances 'no more play today' would have been the order but the authorities decided that a result should be reached if at all possible. The game was to be resolved over 17 overs which meant that Lancashire had to make 98 to win. What followed was a mockery of the game. Class batsmen such as Clive and David Lloyd, Barry Wood and Farouk Engineer were in turn sliding around in the mud, swinging hard to each delivery with no real hope of solid connection. As the rain returned the only player to keep his cool was Keith Boyce who, treading warily up to the wicket, reduced his pace, bowled straight and kept the ball well up to the batsmen. In a little over seven overs he had been presented with eight wickets, but to me it was only a further illustration of how misleading figures can sometimes be.

Two bowlers who returned the identical figures of 7 for 15 are well worth a mention. It is just about 10 years ago that Alan Dixon of Kent mesmerised the Surrey batsmen in a wonderfully controlled exhibition of high class swing bowling at the Oval on a good pitch, and as a result gave his side an overwhelming victory in the Gillette Cup. Two years later Richard Hutton of Yorkshire required only 46 balls to wreck completely the Worcester image at Leeds in a John Player match after Yorkshire had made 183. It is obvious that the batsmen must always take the honours in one-day cricket.

Consider the fact that on Sunday afternoons a batsman can spend two hours in the middle whereas the rules decree that the bowler is only allowed at the most to bowl for approximately 25 minutes. It is therefore the exception rather than the rule when a bowler makes the headlines.

Best Ever One-Day XI

Cricketers and their supporters of all ages throughout the years have passed many satisfying hours selecting best ever cricket teams. I have listened to discussions on best ever sides in school playgrounds, cricket club bars and Test match dressing rooms and so very often have been surprised at the varied permutations put forward. The professional deliberations of our own International selectors so often come in for heavy criticism that no matter how confident I might feel in finally announcing my best ever one-day cricket XI, I know very well that there will be many with valid points to make who will strongly contest my selection.

At least I cannot be accused of prejudice towards the county of my birth or even my adopted county, as I could find no place for any player from the great counties of Yorkshire or Surrey. The first aim was to pick a side that would be effective in all types of one-day cricket, from the 40 overs of John Player League to the 60 overs of a Gillette Cup match.

At least few sane people would argue with the statement that the only real place to bat in a limited-over game is first, and the majority of the most successful one-day batsmen are the openers as a result. One cannot easily forget the exploits of such fine stroke players as Roy Marshall and Bob Barber and more recently John Jameson and Dennis Amiss, whilst Yorkshire have relied almost exclusively on the fine performances of Geoff Boycott and John Hampshire. Remembering how Majid Khan took apart the England attack with a most brilliant Prudential century at Trent Bridge, makes the decision to leave him out a difficult one.

I do not believe that there is a better opening batsman in any form of cricket than Barry Richards and he automatically takes the No. 1 position. The choice of his partner rested between Brian Luckhurst and Glenn Turner. The Kent player with a record aggregate in a season's one-day cricket and a brilliant fielder in any position must be a strong claimant and it was no easy decision to come down in favour of Glenn Turner. The New Zealander, another prolific scorer at any level of cricket has, I believe, the edge when it comes to playing the real pace bowlers and will finally emerge as the best batsman his country has yet produced.

There seems to be a West Indian domination surrounding the No. 3 and No. 4 batting order positions, but before looking at them more closely, let it be said that the name of Greg Chappell was not seriously considered as I felt his short spell with Somerset seven years ago hardly gave him the necessary qualification. Test stars Rohan Kanhai, Clive Lloyd, Alvin Kallicharan and Vivian Richards were uppermost in my thoughts and the final selection fell on Kanhai and Lloyd. Sir Garfield Sobers is the greatest all-round cricketer whom I have ever seen, or indeed ever likely to see, but for all that I can find no place for him in this side. If this was a greatest ever collection of Test cricketers he would be an automatic choice but by his own high standards his record in limited over cricket, most surprisingly, is a modest one. His real experience of it all was limited to the time spent with Nottinghamshire, who were despatched fairly smartly from most of the knock-out competitions and round about that time, years of non-stop action were beginning to tell on the great man.

Preference at No. 5 must therefore be given to Mike Procter, latterly a great rival to Gary as the world's No. 1 all-rounder.

Top class all-rounders must always play a big part in one-day cricket and for this reason our next two positions must be filled by players of this type. Six eminent cricketers were in contention – Ray Illingworth, Ted Dexter, Basil D'Oliveira, Asif Iqbal, Tony Greig and Keith Boyce. Once again, I doubt if the last named could be seriously considered in terms of a five- or three-day match but in consideration of his outstanding efforts, particularly in the John Player League, he cannot be left out. Boyce was the first man to achieve the double of 1000 runs and 100 wickets on Sunday afternoons and his bowling figures of 8 for 26 are still a record for the league. Recalling the early efforts of Ted Dexter, the wonderful consistency of Basil D'Oliveira and the brilliance of Asif, it is difficult to cast them aside but my selection of Ray Illingworth is made in the belief that, whilst captaincy plays a vital part, he would be on hand with the bat should a collapse occur and his bowling would give a better balance to the side.

I have seen no more effective wicket keeper/batsman in many long hours of watching instant cricket than Roger Tolchard of Leicestershire. Alan Knott keeping as skilfully as ever does not have a great one-day record as a batsman and though Farouk Engineer has some stirring performances to his name, the inventiveness of Tolchard with the bat, in my view, secures his place.

Three bowlers are now required to complete the eleven and the first of these must automatically go to Derek Underwood, whose wonderfully accurate left arm spin bowling puts him head and shoulders above any of his rivals. Tom Cartwright, a real specialist bowler in one-day cricket, gives the impression that he must have been born with this type of game in mind. As a medium pacer it has been refreshing to see him constantly attacking the batsman with late movement off the seam without ever losing his unerring accuracy. The search for a pace bowler to complete the attack brought forward the names of Peter Lever, John Snow, Geoff Arnold and Mike Hendrick with the final vote going to John Snow who has been taking wickets, week in and week out, since one-day cricket began and usually at a very low cost. The names of those great bowlers, Trueman and Statham did not come under serious consideration as their playing days had ended around the time that the Gillette Cup was gathering momentum and before the Benson & Hedges Cup or the John Player League came into being. The final side then in batting order reads:

RICHARDS, B.A.
TURNER, G.M.
KANHAI, R.B.
LLOYD, C.H.
PROCTER, M.J.
TOLCHARD, R.W.
ILLINGWORTH, R.
BOYCE, K.D.
CARTWRIGHT, T.W.
SNOW, J.A.
UNDERWOOD, D.L.

There can be few doubts about the batting strength of this side and indeed over 40 or even 60 overs it would be unlikely that nine, ten or jack would need to take guard very often unless wickets were being sacrificed in a late chase for more runs. Snow and Procter would make formidable opening bowlers, with Boyce and Cartwright to follow leaving the spin attack in the capable hands of Underwood and Illingworth. The presence of six front line bowlers covers the contingency of any possible injury.

It is possible that despite the athleticism of Lloyd and Boyce in the field, doubts may be cast on the fielding ability of the above, but one assumes that all are at the peak of their careers which would also mean there is a ready-made substitute wicket keeper in Rohan Kanhai should Tolchard suffer injury.

Barry Richards

Recognition of the point that all great batsmen appear to have that extra little bit of time to play their shots, puts Barry Richards into that elite category. He is able correctly to assess the length of a ball a fraction of a second quicker than most, which in turn allows him to move more quickly into position – this I believe to be the secret of his great success. It is of immense value to him in the one-day game when from the opening ball, he more than anyone else, is confronted with ultra-defensive fields. It has been a revelation to watch him deal so beautifully with the longish half volley directed at his feet. If the predominance of fieldsmen are on the leg side he moves in a flash outside the leg stump and cracks it wide of mid off. When the unfortunate bowler then attempts to strengthen the off side he is perfectly able to bring the orthodox on drive into operation. The value of the speed of his footwork is again illustrated when dealing with the short-of-a-length ball, which so many players are happy to play defensively. Richards again is so quickly into position that he is able to force the ball away off the back foot. Occasionally it brings about his downfall with a catch to the wicket keeper or slip but he gathers so many runs in an arc between deep third man and mid off that he is well on the credit side.

Glenn Turner

To the connoisseur it must have been a fascinating exercise to watch the progress of the New Zealander Glenn Turner. His batting is founded on solid defence and the straightest bat in the game of cricket. He ventured nothing until he felt the base was secure and one-day bowlers were perfectly happy to see him occupying the crease for over after over. Many of them were shrewd enough in fact to try and keep him in. I believe it is fair to say that although Glenn Turner's ultimate ambition was to become a high class Test cricketer he realised before long that he could not be a liability to his County in one-day cricket and decided therefore to use the medium of the limited-over game to cultivate his stroke play. He did this gradually and sensibly and within three or four years there were very few strokes omitted from his repertoire. Important too, was the realisation of the value of the quick single which has subsequently made him into a most efficient runner between the wickets. All in all he stands out now as a complete batsman able to take on bowlers in any form of cricket.

Rohan Kanhai

These days there is a mature look about the batting of the greying Kanhai and only infrequently do we see the odd flashes of brilliance which one time made the Guyanese just about the most exciting player in first class cricket. This is probably born out of necessity rather than desire, as reflexes begin to slow down. He is still a joy to watch but stakes his claim as my No. 3 on the many superlative innings he played in his heyday. Here is a man who in the space of an hour could transform completely any match and change a threatening defeat into an overwhelming victory. On these occasions trying to contain him was just about impossible. How can you keep a man quiet who will cut a good-length ball on the middle stump for four and in almost the same breath hoist a similar delivery over deep mid-wicket for six. This sort of ability is given only to few players. The proud possessor of a string of gold medals in both Gillette and Benson & Hedges Cups for Man of the Match awards, he has passed the three-figure mark in all the major one-day competitions.

Clive Lloyd

The long gangling figure of Clive Lloyd appearing down the pavilion steps is the cue for pints of beer to be quickly drained in the bar and for the bowlers on the field of play to push their fielders another 10 yards deeper. On many occasions for Lancashire he has found himself taking guard when the County has fallen behind the required run rate and it seems to be taken for granted that 'Big Clive' will put things right. More especially on the big occasions he seems to do just that and few will forget those epic performances on Gillette and Prudential Cup Final days. The immense power of his shots, brought about by a full swing of the bat and perfect timing means that any ball beating the field is guaranteed a return of four runs. His ability to push the field deep, opens up the single for him to be taken almost at will and so panther-like is he between wickets that only seven or eight giant strides will see him safely home. If he should happen to strike a co-operative partner scoring six or even seven runs an over appears no great problem. In addition to being a more than useful seam bowler his wonderful fielding ensures that he is normally around 20 runs to his credit before he opens his account with the bat.

Mike Procter

I had the privilege of playing against the two South Africans, Richards and Procter, when as teenagers they toured this country with Wilfred Isaacs XI. In those days Mike Procter, never seriously considered as a bowler, looked the better batsman of the two and even then had a full range of glorious attacking strokes. Suddenly within 12 months of being a third change seamer he found himself spearheading his country's attack and doing it with a large measure of success. Quite possibly his great advance as a bowler of genuine pace and the subsequent calls on his stamina and concentration had some effect on his superb batting potential, but for all that he remained, until a knee injury seriously affected his pace bowling, the outstanding all-rounder produced by South Africa. Those fortunate people at Taunton in 1972 saw an innings of 154 not out made in two hours, including eight sixes and 20 fours in a Benson & Hedges Cup match. Three of the sixes came off successive balls from spinner O'Keeffe. The first one disappeared over the sight screen, the second into the crowd over mid off and unbelievably the hat trick was achieved with an amazing shot over extra cover. No swinging across the line for Procter! If all that was not enough he took the new ball and concluded one of the best all-round performances in one-day cricket with bowling figures of 5 for 26.

Ray Illingworth

Strictly on performance in the one-day game I would not dispute that there are several all-round cricketers with a greater claim to inclusion in this eleven than Ray Illingworth. If Basil D'Oliviera would seem to be an obvious choice then Tony Greig must also have strong claims, along with Asif Iqbal of Kent. My choice of Ray Illingworth was made on two counts.

Firstly, I have been more and more convinced, as the years go by, that captaincy is all important in this type of cricket and secondly the presence of the Leicestershire captain would give the required balance to the attack, and provide the side with a batsman capable of holding the fort should a sudden collapse occur. No one has captained England more skilfully in my time and if anyone would care to suggest that limited-over captaincy requires a very different approach then consider that Leicestershire under his captaincy have been a most successful one-day side. Along with Fred Titmus, Illingworth has been as good an off spinner as we have produced for close on twenty years and his control is such that it is a rare occasion indeed when anyone has really collared him. Twenty-five thousand runs have come from his bat in all types of cricket which surely justifies him as the complete all-rounder!

Roger Tolchard

The choice of wicketkeeper for a one-day game must fall on the person who can also make runs with the bat. Roger Tolchard fills this position admirably. Both Bob Taylor and Alan Knott, could lay claim to having the edge on wicketkeeping ability alone but having said that, let me emphasise that Roger is a fine wicketkeeper in his own right and there would be no place for him in the side if this were not so.

The keeper's job remains a vital one in this form of cricket and is more testing than in the three-day game. With the absence of close fielders the wicket keeper is for ever on the move. Not only has he to be looking to pick up snicks which would normally go to first slip or leg slip, he must be always on his mark to scamper all round the stumps to try and prevent the flow of leg byes which figure prominently in one-day cricket. Tolchard, superbly fit, can take all these demands in his stride and come up as chirpy as ever when his turn comes to bat. His batting indeed has lately been a revelation and there is an unmistakable air of confidence in his approach to the wicket. He has a fine eye, a supple pair of wrists and fleetness of foot which makes him just about cricket's quickest mover between wickets. The quick single is a challenge to him, easy ones are converted into hair-raising doubles and these runs, so upsetting to the opposition, coupled with wristy flicks to the boundary are the basis of his batting. Effective he certainly is, and he continues to surprise many who still underrate him, with the consistency of his performances.

Keith Boyce

Think of the ideal Saturday afternoon professional as a fast bowler, big hitter and brilliant fielder and you have it all rolled into one in the lithe frame of Keith Boyce. I was sitting alongside Trevor Bailey in Barbados on a Cavaliers tour when we first saw him and within 24 hours Trevor, after seeing him bat, bowl and field knew he must sign him for Essex. Since that day he has never looked back and has become a firm favourite on all the Essex grounds. His impetuosity has too often caused his downfall in County Cricket due to his firm belief that every ball should be hit out of the ground, but in the one-day game it has proved most advantageous.

When just a few overs remain there is no one more likely to plunder an attack with a barrage of sixes and fours than Keith Boyce. If his batting remains inconsistent yet spectacular his bowling over the years has greatly improved in accuracy and movement. His great vitality in the field and his natural ability to throw great distances at alarming speed with a low trajectory make that sight of him alone worth the admission money.

Tom Cartwright

Throughout his long career Tom Cartwright had the happy knack of making medium paced bowling look just about the simplest way of making a living in professional sport. In so many ways he has always reminded me of another fine bowler, Derek Shackleton of Hampshire. One has had the impression that they were fully wound up in early May, given a push and through to September they would proceed to drop the ball on an old sixpence without any apparent effort. One-day cricket has produced a breed of very ordinary and negative medium paced bowlers with little talent, parasites of our game and exceedingly boring to watch. Cartwright does not fall into this category. His run up was exactly right, lively, rhythmical and with no flaws. Even into his 40's he retained a splendidly high arm action, a real asset to his bowling. Although I have seen him bowl fine outswingers, it was his sharp movement off the pitch both into the batsman and away from them with little obvious change in action that made him far superior to most of his kind. With this sort of ability he never needed to revert to defensive measures and normally concentrated his attack at the middle and off stump. English pitches, of course, have been of great help to him and there is little doubt that he would have found life much harder if his cricket had been played overseas. An adequate fielder, without ever being outstanding, many will forget that his highest score in first class cricket was 210 for Warwickshire against Middlesex which cannot be bad for our No. 9.

John Snow

The sole Sussex survivor from the first Gillette Cup Final in 1963, John Snow is the last of a quartet of fine hostile fast bowlers. Close on the heels of Tyson, Statham and Trueman he has bowled splendidly in all forms of cricket. He took 3 for 13 on the memorable day at Lords as a 22-year-old and for the last 13 years has been causing problems for the very best batsmen. His extra pace achieved by a really fine body action, coupled with his accuracy and late movement in the air, allow him, in the limited-over game, to start proceedings with a more attacking field than the majority of new ball bowlers. An early breakthrough, of such prime importance, is often the result. His later spell, when operating to a totally defensive field, usually negates the batsman's idea of quick runs. Due to his overs being limited there is seldom any chance of a real haul of wickets and one must appreciate that 4 for 20 is so often a match-winning performance. John Snow has a host of figures such as these to his name and it should be remembered that in recent seasons his County attack has been below strength and consequently he has lacked the support at the other end.

Derek Underwood

Derek Underwood was a boy of 17 when one-day cricket began in earnest in 1963. He duly celebrated its arrival by taking 100 first class wickets that season and set out on an astonishing career which has had few parallels in English cricket. At a time when most spin bowlers are just beginning to find out what it is all about Underwood at the age of 30 is approaching 1500 first class wickets, has already passed the 200 mark in Test matches, has gone well beyond that total in one-day cricket and has pocketed a substantial benefit. He richly deserves all that has come his way and has been a credit to himself and the game of cricket. He has no serious rival for a position in this XI. His method is simple and effective. Masterly control of length and direction and the ability to spin and cut the ball at nearly medium pace make him unplayable on a helpful wicket. On a good batting pitch his control and accuracy make it difficult for any but the most talented of players to force him away. The heave-ho tactics of so many late-order batsmen represent the quickest way of committing batting suicide. Some have been critical of his lack of flight and urged him to toss the ball higher in the style of a Wilfred Rhodes or 'Farmer' White. I have never believed him to be that type of bowler and for goodness sake why should he wish to change from a method which has brought him phenomenal success in the past, with surely hundreds of more wickets yet to come.

Television and One-day Cricket

My debut as cricket commentator on B.B.C.2 took place at Fenners in April 1968. It was an invitation by the producer which took me completely by surprise for never had I considered myself in this role. It had always been in the capable hands of the professional broadcasters such as John Arlott, Brian Johnston and Peter West, but it seemed there was strong support from the then Head of Sport, Bryan Cowgill, that a combination of professional presentation plus deeper cricket knowledge, which can only be acquired by experience in the middle, would improve B.B.C. coverage. That much-beloved character, the late Lord Learie Constantine, had become a regular on Sunday afternoon transmissions, but in his 67th year and leading a very full life, he was only too anxious to dispense with the amount of travelling that is involved in cricket coverage.

I had not bargained for a puncture and a subsequent tyre change en route to Cambridge and arrived with just 10 minutes to spare before play started. Never before had I ever been in a commentary box and for several minutes sat in awe and wonderment at all the technical equipment which surrounded me. Whilst Frank Bough was opening the programme my old friend John Arlott turned to me and said, 'You will be fine – just imagine we are talking together in the saloon bar of a pub, be natural and say whatever you think is right.' It is something I have tried to do ever since.

At close of play I had enjoyed myself tremendously and if I was surprised at the enthusiasm shown by my Producer, I felt I had done sufficient to earn further opportunities. In fact since that day I have missed less than half a dozen B.B.C.2 cricket match transmissions.

The hairiest of all these days happened in that very first year, when the International Cavaliers played Essex at Ilford. Producer, Alan Mouncer, the man who set the format for Sunday afternoon televised cricket, was forever searching for new angles. He thought a new dimension could be added if I combined the jobs of playing and commentating. With some trepidation I agreed and it was also resolved that none of the players taking part should be in on the act. There was, of course, a reason for this as I was to explain to viewers exactly what I anticipated doing with the ball as I ran up to bowl and further discussing the outcome as I walked back to deliver the next ball. I had not foreseen the many drawbacks. A microphone concealed under my shirt with wiring encircling my back connected to a heavy battery in my hip pocket would have made control in my fitter days something of a hazard. At the age of 46 and in nothing like regular practice I would have struggled to survive on a good pitch against a County side without these encumbrances. Without any contact with the Director it was necessary for me to receive a signal informing me exactly when I was to start talking and equally important when I was to stop!

It was finally decided that Neil Durden-Smith, high up in the commentating box would hold high and then drop a white handkerchief as my cue to start talking and would wave it frantically when I was to stop. I picked up the cue immediately and started talking when, to my horror, Fred Trueman, fielding at mid off, converged upon me with several classic Truemanisms which in no way would have gone down well with any cricket-loving spinsters enjoying the cricket in their drawing rooms. I must have looked a sight, with one hand pressed hard over the microphone, trying to negotiate an off spin grip with the ball in my right hand and knowing that I would be completely off balance as I ran in to bowl to Brian Taylor. 'Tonker' Taylor has never been a respecter of persons and with a few old scores to settle I was fully aware I was on a hiding to nothing. Yet I had to tell a quarter of a million people exactly how I proposed getting rid of this volatile left-hander. I remember I began by saying that Taylor's great strength lay in his leg side hitting and policy here would be to bowl on and outside his off stump. No need to say, of course, that my first

ball pitched just about leg stump, and Taylor swinging hard
not only deposited it out of the ground but almost succeeded
in dropping it in the lake in Valentines Park. I really had to
think fast and continued by saying that there was the perfect
illustration of how ruthless a batsman Taylor was with anything pitched around his legs. More by luck than good
management the next ball pitched outside his off stump and
to my great relief he took a single and this uneven contest was
temporarily shelved. At the end of the Essex innings I returned
to the haven of the commentary box fully convinced that with
the great strength of the Cavaliers batting line-up there was
no chance of the No. 11 being required to bat. It seemed that
this assessment was a correct one until a late-order collapse
caused panic stations in the commentary box. Hastily buckling
on pads, slipping in a box, gathering together bat, gloves and
cap and making the frightening descent of a none too secure
ladder in spiked cricket boots I eventually emerged from
behind the screens. As the innings came to a close some ten
minutes later I had cracked three sparkling boundaries and
remained undefeated and only wished I had been equipped
with the microphone when I batted rather than when I had
tried to bowl. Still bowlers have always been the biggest bores
in the business when they happen to make a few runs.

If that exercise had never entirely worked out then it was a
rare blot on the directorship of Alan Mouncer. A brilliant
producer of any sporting programme he established the way
Sunday cricket should be covered, the basics are still there
and there have been few valid criticisms of them. The regular
front man, or link man, for the first half dozen seasons was
Frank Bough and nowhere could one find a more polished or
professional operator. His inborn love of the game of cricket
manifested itself in all his work which, as you may expect, was
carried out with the thoroughness of an expert. He took us on
and off the air without a hitch and was always on hand to fill
in when bad light or rain caused hold ups and delays.

His one embarrassing moment happened on my first day at
Fenners when Lord Butler had agreed to come along to
present the cheque to the winning captain. Frank, in vision,
was closing the programme in his usual flowing manner with
the presentation and as ever was word perfect until to his

horror the name of Lord Butler had gone completely from his mind. 'And here to present the cheque for £50 is,' a pause of only a second or so which must have seemed an age to Frank, 'our very good friend and great lover of cricket.' I know that many people have asked him what flashes through the mind on such an occasion and with a smile Frank has replied, 'My wife, the kids and the mortgage.'

It seemed that when he had to leave B.B.C.2 cricket, which he did with a great deal of regret due to his heavy commitments on Grandstand, Nationwide and other activities, it would be difficult to replace him. The choice of his successor fell on Peter Walker, the former Glamorgan cricketer, who had been making something of a name for himself in South Wales on radio and television and he took to it like a duck to water. Obviously he had a deep and thorough knowledge of the game of cricket, a good command of the English language and equally, if not more important, was a good looking fellow totally relaxed in front of the camera. On the cricket field I always found him completely unflappable and this is a trait he has brought into broadcasting. It is not one of the easiest exercises in the world to close a programme with a 20-second count-down being bellowed in your ear, but to do so on a cricket field surrounded by a hundred screaming youngsters all trying to get in on the act is enough to upset the equilibrium of the majority of people. Peter has emerged from many such scenes with hardly a trace of concern and with still a smile on his face, and continues to handle such situations a good deal better than many with much more television experience.

My constant companion over the last eight years has been John Arlott and no matter how long I had searched through cricket history I could not have found a better colleague. We have travelled countless thousands of miles together on the motorways and byways of our great country. We have enjoyed equally French bread and cheese from the boot of the car and extended dinners into the early hours, and it would be impossible to put a finger on the number of bottles of claret that we have disposed of. In all this time we have hardly had a cross word, plenty of disagreements of course, long arguments indeed, but for all that I continually look forward to our next meeting. Long before we worked together he was firmly established in my mind as cricket's premier broadcaster and my lengthy association with him in later years has simply confirmed this opinion. No one that I have ever met holds the professional cricketer in higher regard than John and hardly ever in his commentary will he have harsh words to say about anyone who makes his living on the cricket field. Apart from his almost insane love of our summer game his other interests are wide and varied.

He speaks with fond memories of his early days in the police force, with great joy of his poetic association with Dylan Thomas, with great enthusiasm on his deep knowledge of the wine industry and with great love for his county of Hampshire. I am sure in the days of steam locomotives he was a walking timetable and knew the Christian names of all the drivers from Waterloo to Alton. One of his finest hours came a few years ago at Trent Bridge one Sunday when heavy rain had suspended play for a good hour and our producer wanted to stay with the cricket scene rather than return to the studio. John immediately offered to go down to the Long Room with a single camera and off the cuff and completely unrehearsed fill in with a talk illustrated with the collection of photographs and trophies on display there, on the history of Nottingham-shire cricket. In company with hundreds of thousands of others I sat enthralled for a good forty minutes during a talk which was superbly presented. I know of no other person connected with the game of cricket capable of such an assign-ment. It must have come as a bitter blow to him when Parr's Tree came crashing down during a winter gale last year.

Former Yorkshire and England captain Norman Yardley knew more about the game of cricket than any man I ever played under. If that qualification did not necessarily make the best captain I have seen, it certainly made him an out-standing 'comments man' on both radio and television. As a cricketer he put one well in the picture with the facts I wanted to know and I have been surprised that he has not appeared more often.

Since its inception the production of B.B.C.2 one-day cricket has been in the hands of three producers. As I men-tioned earlier Alan Mouncer originated the early thinking on format and since then Bill Taylor and Bob Duncan in turn have taken over as Series Producers. In terms of television Bill is a specialist on Rugby Union and Bob is responsible for boxing coverage but the versatility of the B.B.C. producer is such that he is expected at the drop of a hat to be whisked away to cover professionally a sport he knows little or nothing about. As the game of cricket is just about the most intricate and complicated major sport on our screens I could not originally understand how it was possible for a man who knew little about it to make a success of the job. I think Bob Duncan gave me the answer when I discussed it with him, 'I am a television pro – you are a cricket pro – tell me what you want and I will give it to you.' Almost anyone connected with the B.B.C. has more qualifications than I to go into the intricacies of a producer's job and I would not dare to attempt it. I do know that these men are highly trained over many years, some are skilled engineers and expert cameramen, and I have yet to meet one who is not dedicated completely to his profession.

Fixture lists are always a problem and the first headache in the John Player League occurs early each new year when we meet to arrange those matches to be covered on B.B.C.2. Broadly speaking one is looking, if possible, to cover all the Counties over the first 10-week period and concentrate, in the second half of the season, on the sides in contention for the Championship. Ideally one would also wish to give each County a home fixture and similarly be on the look out to take our cameras whenever possible to one of the more picturesque country grounds within the County. Lords, the Oval and Leeds, bear in mind, get a fair saturation of cricket coverage on B.B.C.1 for Test matches. Best laid plans have a nasty habit of coming unstuck especially when you discover that the projected fixture which has been promised for Taunton falls in the middle of a Leeds Test match or indeed a Warwickshire fixture coincides with an England/West Indies Test and you could consequently be left covering a Warwickshire second XI. A lot depends on availability of units and in these days of economical stress and the sharp pruning of B.B.C. costings one has carefully to consider the charges, for instance, of signals and communications for a one-day event. It is therefore considerably cheaper to cover some fixtures than others and even when a reasonable set of fixtures have been drafted they need approval from Lords.

For cricket on B.B.C.1, which involves Gillette, Benson & Hedges and the Prudential one-day fixtures an entirely different team takes over, the team also responsible for Test match cricket. David Kenning who served his apprenticeship under Phil Lewis and Nick Hunter, is the acknowledged king of B.B.C. cricket and has had a great deal to do with the raising of standards of the televised game. David, a more than useful Club cricketer in his day, has been able to combine a sound knowledge of the game with a profound insight into the technical problems associated with the advancement in equipment but, most important, has a natural flair for his job. Life for the director is all about making decisions and moreover, making them on a few seconds notice. Like an umpire, human errors are bound to happen but the better ones make fewer mistakes than their colleagues.

Linking cricket coverage for B.B.C.1, conducting interviews and generally fronting the programme is the familiar face of Peter West. Like all of us Peter comes in for his fair share of criticism, though most of it comes from people who either have never met him or know very little about television requirements. For many years his principal income has come from the media and to maintain a standard of living he has travelled far and wide covering cricket, rugby, dancing, dog shows, circuses, hockey and badminton. You name it and Peter has done it. The Corporation are not fools and if they were not positive that he did not bring professional polish to his various assignments then he would not have been retained. Despite what the public may believe, cricket has always been his first love and he would never let the game down. Probably the finest illustration of his all-round ability occurred during a Lords Test match, when he flew off to Holland on a Saturday evening to give a full commentary on a hockey match between India and Pakistan on the Sunday. We have had problems identifying cricketers from those countries after watching them beforehand but Peter had neither met nor seen any of the 22 players in action that Sunday. According to reports his commentary was faultless, his identification and name pronunciation conducted without an error and at 11.25 a.m. on Monday he was back in front of the camera introducing Test match cricket from Lords.

Almost without exception Australian Test cricketers have regular employment away from the game of cricket. Richie Benaud is by profession a journalist who learned the hard way, as indeed he learned his cricket, which makes his progression to a cricket commentator a very natural one. His success in this field can have come as no surprise to those who know him well, for most of Richie's excursions into commercial life have been successful. I have never met a better organised cricketer or indeed a more hard working one. Within days of his arrival in England in early May until his departure at the conclusion of the Gillette final his diary and working schedule is just about completed. Yet despite this he still finds time to prepare himself most thoroughly and do his homework in relation to cricket commentaries. His brilliance as Australia's captain is forever apparent in his television remarks and he has few peers in assessing a technical situation on the cricket field. Periodically people have questioned the policy of using an Australian to commentate on English domestic cricket. I believe it to be a stupid argument and when it comes, as it has done on occasions from my fellow cricketers, I can only reply that a large percentage of our present-day players first saw the light of day thousands of miles from these shores.

Two great English cricketers make up the commentary team. Denis Compton was the greatest English batsman I ever bowled to and Ted Dexter a superb batsman at his best who I am sure, would have made even a greater impact on our game if he had played in a more carefree period between the wars. It has always been my view that the ex-player, provided he has a reasonable command of the English language, should not have the slightest problem in making constructive observations on a game in progress once he has established a rapport with the Producer. The overriding difficulty is one of continuity. One-day cricket on B.B.C.1 involves a long tiring day with a check-in time of 10 a.m. and normally a 7.30 p.m. finish. One cannot expect the comments man to be in attendance throughout the entire day and in many cases there is not the room anyway. The scorer, with the conglomeration of books and records, a couple of monitors, a stage manager, commentator and the off-duty director, normally would more

than take every inch of available space. Denis and Ted, therefore, can be at a disadvantage in as much that they are not
always fully aware what has been said prior to their taking
over the microphone. Years ago this was not the case, when it
seemed to me that the comments man was only brought into
the act by the ball to ball commentator in reply to a question.
I squirmed in my seat on one occasion when the ball was
turning sharply and the question posed was 'Would you
consider this a turning pitch, Denis?' Very seldom would
either Richie or myself ask a question of Ted or Denis but
simply stop talking when they give us the sign that they
wished to come in. Both of them contribute greatly and probably never better than in the interview position during the
various intervals. They are forthright in their opinion and,
whether you agree with them or not, one can be assured that
they are honest and sincere men.

It would be quite wrong of me to conclude without mention
of the men who work throughout the long day with no relief
in an occupation which demands 100 per cent concentration
and complete accuracy. They are in fact no longer mundane
scorers but highly professional statisticians. Gone are the days
of the old green bound Club scorebook which any member of
the side could take over at a minutes notice. In its place is a
most complex system of scoring, not easy to understand but
wonderfully effective for supplying every possible detail. In
an instant I can be told how many balls Jones has faced in
comparison to Smith, what his score was two and a half hours
earlier, to which part of the field his ninth boundary was
despatched and at what time Green started his second bowling
spell at the pavilion end. In addition to a fund of information
relating to the day's cricket, the scorer is forever noting best
performances and new records, and he provides potted
biographies of all the players taking part. A great deal of
research and a lot of time and preparation goes into these
compilations and the commentator collects many an aggrieved
look if they are not all transmitted!

Obviously statistics play an important part in our coverage
of one-day cricket. I believe it is of great interest to know
something of the background of a young player making his
debut in first class cricket and similar details are most wel-

comed by the commentator when the cricket becomes slow and uninteresting. We must, however, draw the line if and when the statistics become irrelevant, we might otherwise progress to 'And this is the 4000th time that John Edrich has fielded the ball in the gulley since his eldest son was born in Cheam hospital 12 years ago next Tuesday afternoon'.

Roy Webber and Arthur Wrigley were great cricket statisticians in the early days and there have been many who have followed in their footsteps but two in particular stand supreme at the moment. Bill Frindall, in addition to his Radio work is our Sunday afternoon scorer, whilst Irving Rosenwater joins the B.B.C.1 cricket team. Apart from scoring possibly the only thing they have in common is their fantastic love of the game of cricket. I have not seen either of them play the game, but Irving recalls his National Service days when he played alongside Ken Higgs and from all accounts Bill, who has played Minor County cricket, is a more than useful quickish bowler. In my mind's eye I have a picture of the bearded Bill sprinting up to the wicket in an effort to dispose of any surplus energy after being cooped up in a commentary box day in and day out. My chief concern is that they are both extremely knowledgeable and helpful and play a big part in making my work a little less exacting.

How exacting, in fact, is the work and what are the pitfalls? One thing is certain: talking to a cross section of the public which covers anything from a Sunday viewing audience of 2,000,000 to a Saturday afternoon total of 8,000,000 means that you are never going to please everybody. The views of the cricketers themselves listening in the dressing room may well be poles apart from the attitude of the London businessman watching in his West End club. One would have to be fortunate indeed to give pleasure to the members of a working man's club in Wigan and a retired schoolmistress in her Eastbourne cottage. A little while ago I had a complaint from a man in Blackburn who, at great length and in no uncertain terms, emphasised that I had forgotten my Yorkshire upbringing and all my remarks had a distinctly strong Southern bias. In the same post came a letter from Hove saying it might be a good idea if I considered returning to Yorkshire as I had nothing good to say about any Southern cricketer. The only solution was to redirect the letters, sending the one from Hove on to Blackburn and vice versa. I heard no more and for all I know they may still be arguing amongst themselves.

Sitting quietly in the Press Box the cricket correspondent has time to choose his words and assess a situation, whilst few people are in a position to doubt the accuracy of a Radio commentator's report, but on television the commentator must commit himself immediately with the knowledge that any inaccuracies will be immediately spotted by observant viewers. For this reason I have held the view that television work demands a far greater degree of concentration.

Recently I looked for agreement on this point with one of the greatest commentators of all time – Peter O'Sullevan, B.B.C.'s ace race commentator and racing correspondent of the *Daily Express*. It surprised me to discover that he did not entirely share my viewpoint. Whereas he knows that his racing commentary is completely in his own hands and if he should make an odd mistake (which is a rarity indeed) it is his own fault, he can never be certain that his newspaper copy will be faithfully reproduced word for word.

There still remains mixed feelings on the use of the video disc or action replay. Although it means added pressure for the commentator, who remember has already committed himself on the live action, I am sure the action replay, provided it is not overdone, is of great interest. Several people have suggested that it is totally unfair to umpires who have to base their decisions purely on expert knowledge without the advantages of the advanced technical equipment at our disposal. This is a fair argument and is very much in the commentator's mind particularly with regard to a close LBW or a run-out decision but I can recall very few occasions when it had led to any adverse criticism of an umpire's decision. Studied intelligently the action replay can be of great help to the young cricketer, not only in showing the reason for a batman's dismissal, but also for instance in retracing the flowing cover drive of a Barry Richards. One-day cricket seems to need a fuller commentary than a five-day Test match and the long day makes it far more exacting. There is normally more action and consequently more to talk about with constant updating of the situation for thousands of viewers who switch on every few minutes during peak viewing hours.

There can, in my opinion, be nothing to compare with a five-day Test between England and Australia, which even now still pumps the adrenalin, but coverage of our major one-day games continues to be full of interest and is certainly enjoyed by a vast cross section of our cricket-watching public.

Review of the Counties

Derbyshire

In many respects one-day cricket arrived years too late for Derbyshire whose solitary success to date has been to reach the Gillette Cup Final in 1969. If the limited-over game had been in full swing in the early fifties they would surely have been a power in the land. Jackson and Gladwin supported by Bert Rhodes and Morgan would have been a formidable quartet of bowlers and there was never a shortage of batsmen to put bat to ball.

In recent years there has been very little new batting talent and, in general, Derbyshire have experienced one of the leanest spells in their history. For so long many of their stalwarts were recruited from the mining industry when the chance of an open air life with better wages was a great inducement. With improved conditions down the pit and wage increases now far in excess of anything the cricketer earns, it is hardly surprising that new recruits are hard to come by. With falling gates and grave financial reports one sensed an air of desperation in some of the remedies put forward by the committee. In 1972 they persuaded 41-year-old Fred Trueman to play John Player League whilst two more recent signings brought Yorkshiremen Bolus and Sharpe, both in their 40th year, in a vain attempt to bolster the team. If the wisdom of this thinking may well be questioned one cannot help but feel that in contrast they were most unlucky when Lawrence Rowe and Ron Headley arrived at Derby. The brilliant stroke play of the Jamaican had little opportunity to prosper before a serious eye injury caused his departure back home. As yet Ron Headley, though showing glimpses of his true form on occasions, has still not settled down to produce the runs he did for Worcestershire. The real gamble took place as the 1976 season was upon us when Derbyshire succeeded in enticing Eddie Barlow of South Africa over here to play full-time cricket. No one could possibly dispute Barlow's ability but the reported £10,000 salary for four months work would require an awful lot of justification in the South African's performance. Unhappily again for Derbyshire, his record was a modest one but it seemed that he did a great deal to encourage young Geoff Miller and helped him develop from a promising young all-rounder into a Test debutant against the West Indies. The County could also rightly claim that misfortune has continually dogged the efforts of two or three potential bowling aces. I have seldom felt for a bowler more than Bert Rhodes's son, Harold, who carried on for season after season with the stigma of a suspect bowling action undoubtedly caused by an unusual elbow joint. It is no wonder that by the time he was finally cleared he had lost much of his enthusiasm for the game. After an almost sensational start to his career everything turned sour for Alan Ward. It was on the cards that he would have given the Australians the Tyson treatment in 1970-1 but injury caused an early return flight and his difficulties in keeping free of injuries, and mental problems in coming to terms with himself, left his career in a shambles.

It has since been left to Mike Hendrick to shoulder the burden of the Derby attack and there can be few better seam bowlers in the game today. When it seemed that Derby had unearthed at last an England bowler capable of bowling all day under any condition, Mike in turn suffered a couple of nagging injuries which have not been helped by continuing to play when often not fully fit. With the possible exception of Edwin Smith, spin bowlers have always struggled to collect wickets on the green pitches in the County, which made it all the more surprising when Indian off spinner Venkataraghavan joined the club in 1973. A more than useful bowler on the slower yet more responsive Indian pitches, he had to toil hard for a limited amount of success.

If many of their home three-day fixtures are played in front of a mere handful of spectators, there is ample evidence of the intense interest in the one-day game throughout the County.

An enthusiastic crowd filled the delightful Queens Park ground at Chesterfield when our T.V. cameras were there for Sunday cricket, a scene repeated when Darley Dale C.C. was chosen for the important Sunday fixture with Hampshire.

A successful one-day side is surely the answer to Derbyshire's dire financial problems. They really need that little bit of good fortune to enable them to stiffen the batting, for somewhere along the line history may well repeat itself and provide from local talent a brace of big strong medium-quick bowlers who for decades have been the cornerstones of Derbyshire cricket.

Essex

The present Essex C.C.C. was founded in 1876 and since that time the best position they have reached in the County Championship was a third place 80 years ago. The arrival of the one-day game must surely have been greeted with enthusiasm by all concerned with three further opportunities to collect one of the season's trophies. All the more surprising then that an erstwhile Assistant Secretary in 1963 should make the local paper headlines with the statement 'K.O. Cup – not for us'. Oddly enough his forecast so far has turned out to be 100 per cent correct as Essex have yet to reach Lords for a Gillette or Benson & Hedges final and the best they have achieved in the John Player League was runners-up in 1971 and 1976. The John Player League has always seemed to me the competition well suited to the make up of the side and indeed they have continually threatened to snatch the title, only to be unable to last the pace in the critical month of August. Their efforts on Sunday afternoons have been spearheaded by their West Indian import Keith Boyce and no player in this competition has a better record. The first cricketer to accomplish the double of 1000 runs and 100 wickets, his performance of 8 for 26 against Lancashire must have a good chance of standing for all time. Far and away their most accomplished batsman has been Keith Fletcher and during the summer he has consistently looked to be in a class ahead of his team mates, but it really has been the efforts of his lesser known colleagues, who fall into that category of good County cricketers, who must take most of the credit for the continuing challenge of the County in the John Player League.

Stuart Turner, Brian Edmeades and John Lever immediately spring to mind and Ray East has shown repeatedly that the spinner has a vital role to play in limited-over cricket. From Scotland, Brian Hardie has added solidarity and South African Ken McEwan goes from strength to strength and has been a real joy to watch. No one has worked harder for an Essex success than Brian Taylor. It seemed he was on a hiding to nothing when he took over the captaincy from Trevor Bailey but by the time he called it a day his infectious enthusiasm and encouragement had been largely responsible for transforming the County side, whether batting, bowling or particularly fielding, into a most attractive outfit. In 1975 the name of Graham Gooch appeared in the England side, a gamble quite out of character for English selectors. It was my opinion at the time that it was foolish to throw him in at the deep end against the pace of Lillee and Thomson at their peak. I am sure he is a fine prospect if he is allowed to mature for a season or two in his County side. He is certain to play a prominent part for many years to come.

Why is it then that Essex have nearly always been in contention in the John Player League but have a pretty dismal record in Gillette and Benson & Hedges cricket? The shorter 40-over game admirably suits a side in which just about all eleven players can make their 20's, 30's or 40's in quick time, and their bowlers used in short spells have an accurate and lively approach. With the majority of Sunday field placings some distance from the bat they are able to demonstrate to the full their prowess in the field. They are all nimble movers and many of them could rival the Brooklyn Dodgers with the power and accuracy of their outfield returns.

Unfortunately in the longer 60-over competition they appear to have problems in extending their impetus and need to convert the quick 20's, 30's into 40's, 50's and 60's. Perhaps the expected advancement of Graham Gooch will become an important factor in this respect. Nobody in the game of cricket could possibly wish to be envious of any future honours which may well come their way. Few counties in recent times have managed to balance their budget on a limited income as well as Essex whose members and supporters have remained so loyal and faithful.

Glamorgan

Enthusiastic scenes accompanied Glamorgan's great achievement in winning the County Championship in 1948 and 1969. But there has been little to celebrate in South Wales since one-day cricket took a firm hold in our summer months. It does not take a great deal of reasoning to discover why the Welshmen have been the poor relations in the limited-over game. Their excellent performances in 1969 and before then and more particularly in 1948 were the result of top class spin bowling by order of Johnny Clay, Len Muncer, Jim McConnon and Don Shepherd' supported by some of the greatest close catchers in cricket history. Peter Walker, Alan Watkins and Phil Clift have had few peers in those suicide positions close to the bat. In Surrey's great years in the fifties a combination of the Glamorgan spinners plus Walker and company made even as great a player as Peter May look an ordinary mortal. The advent of limited-over cricket has sounded the death knell of the spinner and the complete absence of specialist short legs and slip fielders. The modern game is built around fast and medium seam bowling and this is a department of the game in which Glamorgan have forever fallen short of the high standard required. If that is a generalisation it is only fair quickly to point out that the medium pace of Malcolm Nash, particularly with the new ball, is always something to watch and in recent seasons he has had more success than most in removing opening batsmen in the first few overs. Apart from the unlucky Jeff Jones, they have never possessed a bowler of any great pace, though hopes are high at the moment that Barbadian import Gregory Armstrong, once he has everything worked out, may fill a much needed position.

Perhaps the intense loyalty of the Welsh towards their national game is also a contributory factor. If by a miracle some of those massive prop forwards had switched their allegiance to the summer game they might well have put as much fear of God into English batsmen as they have done for years to our Rugby half-backs. It is strange that the few who have played both games, such as Willie Jones, have been more of the build of a Barry John or a Cliff Morgan with, of course, the notable exception of Wilfred Wooller.

Then, of course, there was the mysterious ending to the contract of Roy Fredericks at the end of 1974. His subsequent performances in both Test and Prudential cricket for the West Indies can only confirm what a major error this has been. He was an ideal foil to the ever dependable Alan Jones and with Majid to follow gave Glamorgan a formidable trio to act as a base for the younger promising talent. Now Majid has gone for good and the manner of his going was sudden and unfortunate. I always have had the impression that all he really wanted to do was to play cricket in his own brilliant and inimitable fashion and had no wish to be involved in local cricket politics. As captain he had to be involved, his cricket suffered, he soon had his fill and quietly packed his bags and left.

Thus the absence of Fredericks together with the retirement of Tony Lewis, Don Shepherd and now Majid have left a void no side could expect to fill readily.

If these problems are not sufficient in themselves Glamorgan geographically speaking must remain at a disadvantage, especially when it comes to Sunday cricket. I recall a few years ago covering Sunday cricket at Buxton when Glamorgan were the visitors. The game took place during a County fixture at Cardiff and after a long day in the field the Welshmen were faced with this long and difficult journey which was hard enough but through some misunderstanding they had no accommodation booked. Although this was finally resolved it was little wonder that Glamorgan were not at their best either mentally or physically on the field that afternoon, more so with the thought of a return journey of another 200 miles that same evening.

At this point in time it would be difficult to foresee any outstanding successes in the near future in relation to limited-over cricket in South Wales but it would at the same time be foolish to underestimate a side which has continually surprised the odds-on favourites.

Gloucestershire

I suppose that all first class cricketers at some time or other during their career cast their eyes at other County sides and think what their alternative choice of County might have been. If I had not been fortunate enough to play for one of the greatest County sides of all times, I think without hesitation I would have plumped for Gloucestershire. They have always been well endowed with attractive stroke makers, a good balance in their attack and plenty of variety of pitches at Bristol, Cheltenham, Gloucester etc. Their victory over Sussex in the 1973 Gillette Cup Final, principally the work of their three leading all rounders, Mike Procter, Tony Brown and Roger Knight gave them their first major success for 96 years, scant reward indeed for the pleasure they have given to countless thousands over the years.

At first glance and at least on paper Gloucester with three Test cricketers appearing in the first five in the order would appear to have an ideal base for quick scoring in a limited-over game. More especially when these three players are Pakistanis Sadiq Mohammad, Zaheer Abbas and the magnificent South African, Mike Procter. Closer inspection would show that Sadiq has taken some little time to sort himself out but over the last couple of seasons he has improved out of all recognition and merits an equal ranking with his illustrious brothers. Gloucestershire must also have had serious doubts about the ability of Zaheer who seemed to reserve his best efforts for Pakistan against England.

Two hot dry summers saw him emerge as not only his County's leading batsman but also the most prolific run scorer in English cricket. The County sadly missed the services of Procter when he was out of action with a serious knee injury brought about by his pace bowling. It must remain a matter of conjecture as to how brilliant a batsman Procter may have been if he had concentrated solely on this department of the game. As it is, it is probably sufficient to say that his arrival at the crease always seems to coincide with even the most cynical Pressman sitting up and taking notice. With so many of the side growing older together there were bound to be countless opportunities for the younger element headed by Foat, Dunstan, Stovold and Hignell. Of these four, Andy Stovold and Alistair Hignell appear to be the pick and it seems likely that with the necessary continued improvement they should figure prominently in West Country cricket in the future.

On the bowling side the cupboard looks distinctly bare. It seems there is little chance that we shall see Procter sprinting in again from his long run and with Tony Brown almost at the end of his career it leaves only Davey, Brain and Shackleton to look after the seam bowling. Jack Davey can be relied upon to plug away and pick up the odd wickets without ever looking a match winner. Brian Brain after a chequered career with Worcestershire, remains an extremely useful new ball bowler, but at 36 years of age he can be regarded only as a short-term investment and John Dixon, if he can find more control over length and direction should be a sounder long-term bet. If there is some similarity in the action of Julien Shackleton and his father, he has still a long way to go to reach the immaculate standards of the old Hampshire bowler. Since the war Gloucester have produced a great line of top class spinners, including Tom Goddard, Sam Cook, Brian Wells, David Allen and John Mortimore, but here again limited-over cricket has taken its toll and it has been left to the lone figure of David Graveney to supply the spin. It has in fact been interesting to watch the young slow left hander go about learning his trade in the most difficult conditions of all for a slow bowler and gratifying to note that he has done pretty well. His father, and more famous uncle, were great competitors and he too has a tough and resilient outlook which will pay off for him.

Gloucestershire too have had their share of captaincy problems and the turn round rate has made even a fourth division soccer manager's job look secure. In the end they made the correct choice in Tony Brown and for eight years he has brought class and quality on the many occasions when his side disintegrated around him. His successor will have a tough assignment, for although financially the County are now breathing a little easier, there is still a number of weaknesses in the side which makes it hard to foresee too much joy for their supporters in the near future.

Hampshire

It came as no surprise to anyone when Hampshire finally
carried off the John Player League trophy at Darley Dale in
1975. The real surprise has been their lack of success in one-
day cricket prior to this, as for some time they had been
knocking on the door in all the competitions. In all probability
the shortage of a pace bowler of real penetration had been a
serious shortcoming but the arrival of Andy Roberts gave the
required edge to their attack. Up to this point it had been
their prolific run scoring in quick time which had given them
a decided advantage over most other sides.

As the years go by one is apt to forget the contribution made
by Roy Marshall, a fine natural cricketer who throughout a
long and distinguished career kept firmly to the theory that
the half volley was there to be hit no matter the circumstances
under which it was bowled. Few sides would seriously contemplate replacing a player of his calibre overnight, yet
Hampshire went a stage further when Barry Richards took
over the mantle of the West Indian. I cannot believe I have
seen a better player anywhere in the world over the last 10
years. It is difficult to assess the heights he might well have
reached had he for instance been born an Australian. As a
South African he has been unable to exploit his great talent
to the full at the highest level but if the opportunity had been
there I am sure, the very competitive nature of the game at
Test Match standards would have made him an even greater
player. In the company of coloured cricketers in the Cape
recently it was most interesting to learn that in their view
Barry had worked harder than any South African to encourage
multi-racial cricket in his own country.

The very nature of Gordon Greenidge's approach to batting
must make for inconsistent spells yet there have been several
occasions in the one-day game where he has matched Richards
ball by ball and when this has happened the outcome of many
of the fixtures has been a foregone conclusion very early in
the piece. Pity then the position of David Turner with the
unenviable task of following these two, though a glance
through the record books would show how well he has done
and I am sure we have not yet seen the best of him. Trevor

Jesty is proving an invaluable all-rounder and may well make an M.C.C. tour before long. Hampshire moved very smartly when for some unaccountable reason Nottingham did not re-sign Mike Taylor and he has proved to be a particularly shrewd acquisition. The same can also be said of 'keeper Bob Stephenson who moved down from Derby whilst Bob Herman, a Middlesex reject, has collected useful wickets for them.

No side can be successful without a couple of characters who seem to rally the team when the chips are down and there are few better examples than Richard Gilliat and Peter Sainsbury. The veteran Sainsbury has been one of my favourite cricketers for 20 years. The real life blood of our first class game. Utterly reliable, a man who has extricated his side from many a tight corner with the bat, has bowled his overs economically, taken vital wickets in match after match and capped it all with brilliant work in the field. When the champagne has been flowing and the crowds cheering it seems he cannot really understand what all the fuss is about.

Richard Gilliat is certainly the most underrated captain/batsman in the country and has certainly deserved more recognition than has thus far come his way. A high intellect does not always make for a good cricket captain but Richard has led the Hampshire side for the past six seasons in an extremely competent manner, quite apart from his excellent record with the bat.

One could query Hampshire's immediate prospects with Barry Richards' cricket future still in doubt, the question mark as to how long Andy Roberts can keep up his blistering pace and the imminent retirement of Peter Sainsbury. For the County to remain as challengers for one-day cricket honours, a top class pace bowler and a spinner would seem to be their first priority.

Kent

No county has had more all round success in one-day cricket than Kent. Gillette Cup winners in 1967 and 1974, winners of the John Player League in successive years, 1972 and 1973, and in the latter year making it a double with the Benson &

Hedges Cup. If that was not sufficient they completed the double again last year, coupling their Benson & Hedges success with a late and dramatic victory to give them another Sunday championship by the minutest of fractions. It is also probably fair to say that if the side had not been seriously depleted with Test match calls and persistent injury problems, their ratio of success would have been greater still.

The reason for their run of success is not difficult to establish with nine Test match cricketers making up a powerful combination, four of whom are international all-rounders in their own right. In common with the other successful one-day sides they have great depth of batting and it seems almost farcical that on occasions, Julien, Shepherd and Woolmer should occupy the seven, eight and nine berth when one considers that Shepherd boasts a top first class score of 170 and the other two have made centuries for their respective countries. It may be surprising, therefore, that none of the three mentioned have scored heavily or consistently in the limited-over game, a factor which also applies to Alan Knott. Invariably, of course, they are committed to sacrificing their wickets in the chase for runs after the foundation has been successfully laid by Messrs. Luckhurst, Johnson, Denness and Cowdrey.

Possibly one does not associate Colin Cowdrey with a method of play vital to one-day cricket but one cannot lose sight of the fact that he has collected the Gillette 'Man of the Match' on no fewer than five occasions. Watching Brian Luckhurst open in a three- or five-day match one may well be excused for putting him in the same category and how wrong you would be. No batsman, in my knowledge, has adapted himself better to the needs of one-day cricket. In 1974 he scored 1061 runs in limited-over cricket, the first batsman to do so and I will long remember him taking apart Tom Cartwright of all people in making a score of 142 at Weston one Sunday well within the 40-over limit. He now goes into retirement and paves the way for Bob Woolmer to take over his role.

The talented Graham Johnson and skipper Mike Denness seldom fail, whilst the cheerful Asif Iqbal is always a joy to watch. There is no question that it is vital to bat early in the order to make a consistent impact and Kent could possibly have won the John Player League with nine players drawing lots weekly for a batting position. Collecting seven trophies in the past nine seasons one may well wonder why the County Championship has only come their way on one occasion since the war. I am sure the answer is related to the fundamentals of the two games.

To win the County Championship one needs to bowl out the opposition twice; to win the limited-over game one needs only to contain them. If the Kent attack has lacked the necessary penetration on good wickets, they possess in Woolmer and Underwood two highly skilled bowlers who with their unerring accuracy cause frustration to all but the greatest one-day stroke makers. In support are the West Indians Julien and Shepherd and that awkward customer Norman Graham whose efforts so often have been unappreciated.

One could not conclude any discussion on Kentish achievements without mentioning the name of Alan Ealham. I am never unduly concerned if one of the stars is absent when our T.V. cameras go down to Canterbury provided the name of Ealham is on the team sheet. We are then assured of a brilliant display of outfielding, usually in the vicinity of the famous tree, a running catch to leave one speechless and so often the sight of a returning batsman sadly shaking his head in disbelief when the second run seemed there for the taking.

With Tavare looking a player of real class, another Cowdrey about to make his mark and Jarvis a brisk bowler in the making, the Kent side remains young enough to be a power in the land for some time to come and it will be surprising if further honours do not come their way.

Lancashire

From the outset it seemed likely that Lancashire would play a prominent part in any form of one-day or limited-over cricket. They have carried off the Gillette Cup on four occasions since its inception in 1963 and have twice been successful in winning the John Player League.

The majority of their staff have been expertly initiated into the techniques of afternoon cricket from a tender age in the

22 Ray Illingworth – master technician with a fine action.

23 Roger Tolchard. A real 'one-day' specialist.

24 Barry Richards. Who wants to bowl next?

25 *Left* Underwood. Another 'deadly' special on its way.

26 *Above* Mike Procter. Pace bowler and punishing
   batsman. The envy of our selectors.

27   John Snow allowing himself 'poetic licence' with the no-ball law!

28   *Right, above* Medium pacer Cartwright displaying perfect balance and superb body action.

29   *Right* Canterbury. Enthusiastic scenes even on a two-sweater day.

30 *Top* Greig, c Marsh b Gilmour. Who needs slip fielders?

31 *Above* The Fenner Trophy brings the crowds to the
Scarborough Festival.

most competitive form of cricket in the country – the Northern Leagues. This has been most evident in so many aspects of their approach to the game. Their successes in the 60-over game particularly when batting second have been a revelation on how to time a run chase. They always look for a sound start from Lloyd (D.), Wood and more recently Engineer, and appreciate the value of a solid base even if it seems, to their anxious supporters, that they are slipping perilously behind the required run rate. It is, of course, an enormous advantage to them that waiting in the wings are the diminutive Pilling, the enigmatic Hayes and the brilliant Clive Lloyd, each of whom can win a match off his own bat.

Even then they are far from finished with David Hughes and Jack Simmons to follow. As long as one-day cricket is played at Old Trafford the name of David Hughes will last forever as a result of his match winning performance in that 10-hour epic against Gloucestershire in 1972. And what a valuable cricketer Jack Simmons has turned out to be. Thirty years of age before he was awarded his cap, his years as professional at Blackpool and the experience gained there have made him a vital cog in the Lancashire machine. A mean and niggardly bowler, as difficult to get away as any of his type, a late-order batsman who can switch from defence to attack and a fine collector of half chances at slip, have made him an automatic choice.

Lancashire too have the ideal balance in attack to ensure success on all types of pitches. The pace of Peter Lever, the controlled movement of Lee and Wood, the useful seam bowling of Clive Lloyd, the accurate spin of Hughes and Simmons and, in reserve, the promising newcomer Ratcliffe. Most important of all, as far as one-day cricket is concerned, is that Wood, Clive Lloyd, Hughes and Simmons can be classified as genuine all-rounders which gives the required depth to batting and bowling and is the envy of so many other counties. No fewer than 10 of their players have collected 'Man of the Match' awards – a statistic which speaks for itself.

The Lancashire committee were shrewd enough, some years ago, to appreciate that the arrival of one-day cricket was going to be the principal factor in solving the County's financial problems during a very lean time in their history. It was vital that they started winning and quickly, and I am convinced that the signing of Clive Lloyd and Farouk Engineer were effected with one-day cricket in mind. It has paid off handsomely with upwards of 25,000 people filling the great cricket ground and bringing an atmosphere which has been a revelation to us all.

In 1976, I had, for the first time, a feeling that their strength was on the wane, but it is difficult to say whether this was due to the absence of Clive Lloyd. Their supporters will certainly say that his absence was the sole reason for their losing their firm grip on the Gillette Cup.

The impending retirement of Lever and Engineer will make life difficult for them particularly as Kennedy, Abrahams and Reidy are struggling to make the grade. It would be foolish to say that the boom time is over for them, particularly with the return of Clive Lloyd, but I still harbour a few lingering doubts. '

Leicestershire

The resurgence of Leicestershire cricket in recent years has given enormous pleasure and satisfaction to cricket followers all over the country. Their success in both the John Player League and the Benson & Hedges Cup, has played an important part in helping them finally to carry off the County Championship for the first time in their 97 years' history. Between the wars they produced a host of fine cricketers, too numerous to mention, and in more recent times, when Surrey were having their phenomenal Championship run, points were always hard to come by at Grace Road. In contrast to the thriving city itself, there was no affluence in evidence on the ground itself. The dressing-rooms in the old ramshackle pavilion were ill-kept, with rickety steps leading down to a solitary basement shower where if one was lucky there might be a spray of ice-cold water. Luncheons were just about palatable and conditions generally primitive for the small crowds that came along. If the pitch was normally hard and flat, the outfield was in direct contrast, and a high percentage of players found it necessary to wear a box when in the field. It seemed then that Leicestershire would be lucky to survive their financial problems.

What a transformation, therefore, has taken place in the last decade. Modern and comfortable changing rooms in the new pavilion wing, greatly improved catering facilities, an abundance of hospitality, a thriving Supporters Club and a lush green and grassy outfield. The leading role in this revival has been played by the Secretary, Mike Turner, who was clever enough to realise that the support and sponsorship he gained through local industry would not survive without success on the field itself. Leicestershire had always produced three or four excellent home products, but it was obvious that they had to import other players to give the side the required balance. The signing of Tony Lock on a three-year contract in 1965 marked the early beginnings of the County revival and his departure to Australia coincided with the arrival of Ray Illingworth and Graham McKenzie. The partnership of Turner and Illingworth prospered from the outset, both were quick to realise that, however one might cherish the County Championship pennant, one-day cricket was more likely to boost the gates and bring bigger financial rewards to the players themselves. To this end they persuaded the admirable Ken Higgs to return to first class cricket, they saw the drawing power of the exciting young Rhodesian Brian Davison and realised the one-day potential of their young wicketkeeper/batsman Roger Tolchard. Balderstone and McVicker subsequently followed to join the ever improving Dudlestone and John Steele and veteran Micky Norman was always on hand to steady the ship.

Illingworth's job was to weld together a combination of highly experienced (if slightly ageing) Test cricketers with a couple of County rejects and young potential talent and no one could have done the job better. He saw no reason why the slower bowlers should not play their part and through the years has on many occasions used Balderstone, Birkenshaw as well as himself to bowl their full quota of overs.

Leicestershire's success in one-day cricket, therefore, can be attributed to fine leadership, the accuracy of their seamers and the ability of the spinners in a side not restricted in the number of bowlers they can turn to. No less than eight regular bowlers have turned out weekly, and that has carried them through Test match calls and injury problems. Consistency rather than brilliance has seen them through with the bat in an order with sufficient depth to make sure they will invariably score steadily if not heavily.

The retirement of McKenzie and the fact that Higgs cannot have too much more cricket to look forward to, means that Leicestershire desperately require a new young pace attack if their success is to continue. Peter Booth has yet to fulfil his early promise but when Alan Ward suddenly became available after yet another upset with Derbyshire, Mike Turner was quick to snap him up. Possibly a change of scenery will do him good and if he can stand the strain of a hard season he could turn out to be just what Leicester require. Add to this their highly organised youth coaching scheme and their uncanny knack of picking up the strays, helping to balance the side in which the up and coming youngsters such as Gower, Briers and Clift will surely make their mark, and they must remain a power in the land.

Middlesex

Arguments have raged over the years as to the value of playing all one's home fixtures at the headquarters of cricket, where most of the people that count spend the majority of their time. One thing is certain – it has not been of much help to Middlesex who, though threatening on occasions, have thus far been unable to win any one-day competition. There are normally no half measures about the County's performances and it seems they either completely overwhelm the opposition or alternatively go under by an equally big margin. Whatever people may believe, there are always added pressures when playing at Lords. One can look forward immensely to turning out there two or three times a year but playing there regularly has, I am sure, affected many young players in particular and has been a prime reason for the failure of several of them to realise their full potential.

To their eternal credit Middlesex continue to believe in the value of the spinner in the one-day game. Admittedly in the shape of Fred Titmus they have the finest bowler of this type in the club's history who would have been a star in any

County, no matter what the competition. At the same time they have encouraged Phil Edmonds to bowl his regular stints and have begun to groom the off spinner John Embury as a successor to Fred Titmus. There might well have to be some re-thinking in this respect in view of batsman Norman Featherstone's sudden emergence as a valuable additional spinner. It is to be hoped that Edmunds' future as a Test Match bowler will not be jeopardised by attempting to change his style to suit limited-over cricket. On several occasions it seems he has been instructed to bowl 'à la Underwood', that is, pushing the ball through at almost medium pace, aiming around middle stump. Four cheap wickets on a Sunday afternoon is poor recompense if it materially affects the long term chance of a haul of Test Match wickets. Indeed, could his surprising omission from the M.C.C. side to India be attributed to this?

The retirement of John Price left a gap that has been very hard to fill and though he returned to help out in one-day fixtures, it is never easy even for the top liners to reach the standards they had attained with regular practice. Ted Dexter and Fred Trueman would surely agree.

My first sight of Martin Vernon in a Benson & Hedges match at Hove was a most encouraging one but since then he has failed to maintain the pace he showed that day. The arrival of Wayne Daniel will be eagerly awaited by all at Lords and provided he is able to stand up to the demands of an English season, he should make his presence felt. With the great improvement of Mike Selvey, some lively and spirited bowling from Alan Jones and the useful Tim Lamb in reserve, Middlesex indeed have an embarrassment of riches which leads one to believe that someone is going to be desperately unfortunate to be omitted. Already the County have dispensed with the services of Test player Larry Gomes and given preference to their second overseas player, Norman Feather-stone. On the face of it Gomes looks a better cricketer but Featherstone, five years a capped player, gives the side a better balance. Together with Featherstone the task of scoring runs has largely been left to the hard core of Mike Smith, Clive Radley and skipper Mike Brearley. To these names can now be added two of England's future hopes, Graham Barlow and Mike Gatting. This side really is becoming just about the most powerful outfit in the country.

Since the days of R.W.V. Robins, Middlesex seem to have had a strange collection of captains and Mike Brearley's agreement to take on this job must have been welcomed with open arms. Despite many frustrations he has done his job well, well enough in fact for many to believe he was somewhat unfortunate not to take over the England side when Ray Illingworth stepped down. In 1975, John Murray, prince of wicket keepers and a most elegant batsman, decided to call it a day. Highly respected in every part of the world, his contribution to Middlesex cricket goes without saying and as one of cricket's finest ambassadors, he will be sorely missed.

It is not surprising then that the 1976 County champions must go forward as the side that everyone has got to beat. If they are not in contention for each and every one of our major competitions over the next few years, a lot of searching questions should be asked at Lords.

Northamptonshire

For so many of the pre-war years, Northants were stuck with the label of the poor relations of County cricket. Always, provided the opposition could quickly dismiss that fine and elegant batsman, Dennis Brookes, and then overcome the fiery pace of 'Nobby' Clark, the chances were that they would be on their way with a day to spare.

The registration of overseas players, an easing in the laws of inter-County players transfers and the arrival of the one-day game, has brought an air of change in Wantage Road. It has not been by any means a rapid transformation. The turning point was in the fifties, with the arrival of Frank Tyson and those two fine Australian cricketers, Jock Livingston and George Tribe, ably assisted by Keith Andrew, surely one of the most accomplished wicket keepers in my playing time. If the side of this particular era did not collect any championship prizes they helped immeasurably to increase confidence all round and begin to put Northants back on the map. Tyson and Tribe, both back in Australia, Livingston now domiciled in Sussex and Andrew doing sterling work back in his native

Lancashire, must have raised their glasses high on 4th September 1976. At around 7 p.m. their Pakistani captain, Mushtaq, hoisted the Gillette Cup aloft and after all the long years of waiting Northants had beaten Lancashire, of all people, and the break through was finally accomplished. The side that completed this memorable performance consisted of three players from Durham, two from Pakistan and one each from India, Yorkshire, Kent, Staffordshire, Somerset and Bedfordshire which amply illustrates the dearth of local talent in Northamptonshire. Staffordshire and Durham have appeared to have been the principal recruiting grounds for them, and nobody made a greater impact from the North East than Colin Milburn. It was highly probable that they would have won a major award a little earlier if Colin's career had not been horribly curtailed by that tragic car accident. Here was a man born for one-day cricket and Northants lost him at a time when their very need was for an attacking opening batsman.

Thus they went through an interim period of trying out promising youngsters who never quite make the grade. Roy Virgin acquired from Somerset gave them the solidity they required but it was only when Peter Willey was promoted to join him that they began to blossom.

Nothing gave me greater pleasure in 1976 than a glorious Willey century at Bradford and his fine performances in the Gillette semi-final and final. I felt it was verging on lunacy when he was omitted from the M.C.C. tour of India. With Mushtaq to follow and two very bright prospects in Geoff Cook and Wayne Larkins, the Northants batting, which has previously looked uncertain, seems a whole lot healthier.

There can be few doubts about the bowling strength provided they can find a replacement for Bob Cottam who has served them so well since his transfer from Hampshire. Even Kent could ill-afford to release a bowler of John Dye's ability and John who continues to give all he has every minute of the day, was a master signing. Sarfraz looks what he is, every inch a Test Match bowler and has the happy knack, uncommon to most of his kind, of dismissing good players on good pitches. Incredibly Northants have been reluctant to play Bishen Bedi in a vast number of one-day games. Whilst Bishen has a mind of his own and quite rightly refuses to prostitute his art by bowling flat and defensively, he surely has sufficient skill and perception to be successful whatever mode of cricket he plays in. Larkins with seam bowling and Peter Willey whose bowling of off spinners may well show a vast improvement over the years, make up a well balanced attack.

The only aspect of the side which is likely to count against them is their fielding. They have to carry three or four passengers in the field. This was always a possibility in the old days, but in limited-over cricket, there is simply nowhere to hide and I believe an all-out effort should be made to improve this department. Still they now know what it is like to win something. The break through has been made and there is no reason why their success should not be repeated again before very long.

Nottinghamshire

Cricket records show all too readily a nil return for the once famous County of Nottingham in one-day cricket, though at last the season 1976 provided sound evidence that the decision to concentrate their efforts on unearthing local talent was the correct one. Prior to this they had proved the old theory that no one man can make a cricket team, even if he is the greatest all-rounder the game has ever seen. In fairness to Gary Sobers, he was worn out with cricket when he arrived at Trent Bridge and the edge of his fitness, so vital to his style of play, had begun to fade. Of course there were magical moments but few real glimpses of his greatest and really the Notts gamble did not work out. I would never quarrel with Nottinghamshire over the Sobers' signing as I felt it was a calculated risk well worth taking, but I could never understand the appointment of the 42-year-old Jack Bond as manager/captain nor indeed could I understand the Lancashire captain accepting it. It is history now that it turned out to be an abysmal failure and is best forgotten – but it led to some fresh thinking at Trent Bridge. The captaincy was handed over to one of their leading batsmen, the level-headed dependable Mike Smedley and a big drive around the County was put in progress to try and discover young cricketers for the future. With a vacancy for an overseas cricketer to augment the home grown talent, Nottinghamshire lowered their sights a little and brought over Clive Rice from Johannesburg. Little-known in this country he has made a most promising start and looks a valuable acquisition.

The backbone of the batting for some time has been the solid figure of Mike Harris and his willingness to take over behind the stumps to best suit the needs of his side, has made his contribution even greater. That most engaging Kenyan, Basharat Hassan, has enlivened many a day at Trent Bridge and has an excellent one-day record. His most recent partner Paul Todd appeared with all the requisites of the limited-over batsman and has already made a number of bowlers sit up and think. The promise of greater things to come has fallen on the slim shoulders of another local boy, Derek Randall. He announced his arrival five years ago at the age of 20 with a flurry of sixes against Essex and was hailed as an England batsman almost before his first bat was broken in. For three seasons now he has been discovering what this game is all about and with a number of responsible, yet highly entertaining, innings under his belt he could be the man to lead in the rebuilding of the County's cricket future. As a cover point fieldman he has few equals anywhere in the world.

Dismissing the opposition reasonably cheaply or indeed containing them has never been easy despite the efforts of paceman Barry Stead and spinner Bob White, both of whom have done an admirable job. The former has been a consistent wicket-taker whilst Bob White, with few chances in his Middlesex days, must have surprised many Londoners with a number of fine returns since he left Lords. The new crop of youngsters now appearing in the side include Peter Johnson, a former Oxford blue, John Birch, Trevor Tunnicliffe and Philip Wilkinson and for their side to begin a forward march much depends upon them. Memories of closed gates for County matches at Trent Bridge and the great friendliness of the welcome afforded there to so many of us has established that delightful ground as a firm favourite for many years. It has been sad to watch a County with a great history and a succession of wonderful cricketers languishing in the wrong half of the table. The industry and imagination of the secretary and committee have succeeded in making the arena commercially viable and in keeping with modern requirements. They desperately need success on the field to make it all worthwhile. If they can sustain the 1976 improvement, happier days are sure to return to Trent Bridge.

Somerset

One cannot fail to be stimulated after a visit to the County of Somerset, especially after spending an hour in the company of the ageless Bill Andrews. To be a good listener is a prerequisite as he provides a complete run down on the great potentials of young players within the County and in the end one wonders how it is that a solitary appearance in the Gillette Final in 1967 remains their best performance. The enthusiasm of Bill Andrews was echoed by all their supporters on that day at Lords when they appeared clad in smocks, brandished pitchforks and brought their own barrels of cider. A great many people hoped for a Somerset win but after a valiant fight they went under to Kent by 32 runs.

It is quite possible that before very long Somerset supporters will have something to shout about for, I think, there is no doubting the quality of a number of their young cricketers. Slocombe, Roebuck and Marks are three who spring to mind immediately and always provided their progress continues they should have an exciting future. Peter Denning and Ian Botham are now a little more experienced and beginning to prove their worth and Brian Rose should really move on to better things. Only Ian Botham of this quintet is a bowler and it is in this department that Somerset seem to need some stiffening. In addition to this band of youthful talent Somerset can boast a further blend of experienced County players to match their registered overseas cricketers.

The County will welcome the return of the brilliant Viv Richards after his all-conquering performances in a long series of West Indian Test matches. He should not forget the county that gave him the opportunity to develop into one of the game's greatest present-day batsmen.

Hallam Moseley from Barbados has spearheaded the attack and has been a regular wicket taker. Somerset must be well

satisfied with their efforts in persuading Brian Close (Yorkshire), Tom Cartwright (Warwicks.), Derek Taylor (Surrey)
and Alan Jones (Sussex) to move to the West Country. Each
in turn has performed with distinction. Brian Close, one of the
finest of our post-war captains, a veritable Peter Pan of cricket
has a great chance of completing 30 years in the first class
game, a testimony to his fitness and enthusiasm which has
lifted his adopted County on more than one occasion. Tom
Cartwright, over a long and distinguished career, has had few
peers as a bowler in one-day cricket. It was always a great joy
to watch him practising his art. Subtle variations of pace,
consistent movement both ways off the pitch coupled, as
always, with unerring accuracy. If these two seniors have
maintained their performances then Derek Taylor has improved by leaps and bounds. In common with several of my
old Surrey colleagues, I was extremely sorry to see him leave
the Oval where, most unfortunately, he had few opportunities
to further his talents. Regular first class cricket has seen him
develop into one of the most accomplished wicket keepers in
the country and has brought a new note of confidence to his
batting. Although he has now retired, Brian Langford's name
should not easily be forgotten. As a slow off spin bowler he
came to terms with the limited-over game as well as anybody
and remarkably enough was the first bowler to achieve the
ultimate in the John Player League. Eight overs, eight
maidens against Essex at Taunton! I cannot think what was
going through the mind of the non-striking batsman that day
who happened to be Keith Boyce.

One can only conclude with a reference to a true son of the
County who for 10 years has unstintingly given his all without
looking for praise or headlines. Graham Burgess with ball or
bat has always been doing something useful and though never
making the heights of his more illustrious colleagues has been
a very vital member of this extremely useful side. He will be
remembered as a good County cricketer and that, in my book,
is something about which he can be extremely proud. Mervyn
Kitchen comes into the same category and what a great end
to the season it would have been if last year these two, after
leading a Somerset revival, could have added just that extra
run to have given them the John Player League title.

Surrey

Whichever way you look at it, Surrey, one of the leading post war sides in three-day cricket, have been a huge disappointment to their committee and members whenever limited-over cricket has been played. It must be said that they have had sufficient talent in their side during the last decade to have brought them more rewards than winning the Benson & Hedges Cup in 1974.

The batting mainstay throughout has been the redoubtable John Edrich – a model of consistency under all kinds of conditions. Graham Roope, Younis Ahmed and Geoff Howarth also have pretty good records but the performances of such fine stroke players as Stuart Storey and Mike Edwards in the earlier days have really been hard to understand. Few batsmen hit the ball harder than Surrey's popular all-rounder Intikhab Alam, yet he in turn has disappointed with the bat.

Perhaps it has taken Surrey longer than most sides to work out the requirements of the one-day game, particularly in terms of run scoring. One has often come to the conclusion that they have had the mistaken idea that to put together a substantial score it is necessary to crash every ball to the boundary. They have possibly neglected the art of the short singles, or looking to make ones into twos, which always puts pressure on the fielding side. There are very few friendly offerings from professional bowlers and, particularly on Sunday afternoon, one would have to wait an awful long time to hit the bad ball for four. Too often have I seen good Surrey batsmen 'hole out' at deep mid off attempting to force a good length ball when a push and run would have brought a safe single.

If Edrich has been the essence of reliability with the bat then Geoff Arnold has done equally well with the ball. In addition to bowling his overs most economically he has been far and away the most reliable of the Surrey attackers. Robin Jackman has had his moments and one particularly remembers his 7 for 33 against Yorkshire in a Gillette match at Harrogate. The role of third seamer, so vital to this type of cricket, has never been adequately filled. Graham Roope has lacked the penetration and the younger brigade of Butcher, Baker and

Smith have so far been found wanting. Pat Pocock with an increase in pace from his accustomed slow medium off spin has seldom been collared and Intikhab, on two or three occasions, has made life difficult for batsmen. It is indicative of our modern game when one of the leading leg spin bowlers in the world can play several matches without ever turning his arm over.

Few would seriously disagree that from a playing point of view Surrey now have a shortage of players likely to do well. Willis, Selvey, Roger Knight all successful one-day cricketers, have been allowed to slip through their hands. There is a crying need for a good third seamer who could also bat around number six and, in relation to John Player cricket, it has constantly surprised me that no approach has been made to any of the good club cricketers that abound in the County. It is hard to expect a teenage bowler on the staff to fulfil that role and have immediate success. If Surrey could strengthen their side in this respect and greatly improve their whole approach to limited-over cricket, there is no real reason at all why they should not get back on the winning trail.

Sussex

To those whose interest in the one-day game is related only to the last few years, it will come as a shock that Sussex originally were the most feared opposition in the country. Inspired by Ted Dexter they took a firm hold of the Gillette Cup in the early years, winning it in 1963 and 1964, and in fact playing ten of these cup ties before first tasting defeat. So adept were they at this new form of cricket that also in 1963 they took on the full might of the West Indian Test side and beat them handsomely at Hove. Even in later years, when the successful side began to break up and they found themselves struggling for survival in the John Player League and the Benson & Hedges Cup, the word Gillette has acted as some form of inspiration to them as their three subsequent appearances in the Lords final have proved.

Only John Snow has survived over the years from a side which showed the rest of the country how limited-over cricket should be played. Ken Suttle was ideally suited with his unorthodoxy – pushes, tickles and the bat craftily angled, followed by well-timed hitting to leg. He paved the way for those two fine stroke players Jim Parks and Ted Dexter who took the one-day game by storm. With Alan Oakman, the very useful Graham Cooper and Les Lenham continually weighing in with useful scores, they seldom experienced much trouble in reaching a decent total. If Dexter took a few chances with the bat, he took hardly any when his side went out to field. Quick to appreciate that taking wickets was of less consequence than the scoring of runs he made sure that the opposition surveying his shrewd and tactical field placings, would wonder where on earth the runs were coming from. However wise he might have been, it would have been quite useless without the bowlers to support him and they seldom let him down. Ian Thomson in particular did a great job and together with Tony Buss and Don Bates formed an accurate and formidable trio. Dexter completely erased the spinners from his one-day thinking, not that he had much choice with the material at his disposal.

Sussex supporters with these memories behind them are now asking themselves if Tony Greig in the seventies can repeat what Ted Dexter achieved in the sixties. He is patently aware that to do this the side desperately needs some strengthening. His winter travels have seen him negotiating in turn, but unsuccessfully, with Australians Thomson and Gilmour, but it is hard to believe that Sussex could offer the type of reward so readily coming the way of Australian cricketers. He may be better advised to research the home market. It has certainly paid off for Hampshire and Leicestershire. His own efforts will assuredly be of the highest order and he can count on excellent support from his fine left-hander Peter Graves. Roger Knight's move from Gloucestershire has already paid handsome dividends and his punishing blade has had the Hove crowd on their feet on many a Sunday afternoon. John Barclay has shown steady improvement but the find of 1976 was, without doubt, the young Pakistani Javed Miandad. Now here is a player of great talent who will surprise many if he is not shortly making centuries, not only for Sussex but also for his country.

With a benefit behind him, it is now debatable how long

John Snow will continue. Few bowlers have been able to rival him in the one-day game, all of which means he will be a difficult man to replace and it is in the bowling department that Sussex need to look to the future.

The subtle variations of left armer Michael Buss have produced some excellent spells and slow bowler Chris Waller has more than justified his move from Surrey. John Spencer too can be congratulated on extremely accurate bowling, but for all that it seems there is a crying need for another pace bowler of real penetration. Sussex are fortunate that in Tony Buss and Les Lenham they have top class coaches scouring the County for local talent. If they can succeed in finding the fast bowler they need and bring to the fore a couple of their younger batsmen, then Sussex can look forward to a return to their halcyon days of the sixties.

Warwickshire

Any coloured cricketer from the Cape whose lunch consists of a hot pattie eaten out of the paper and whose 20-minute tea break allows him a bottle of highly coloured mineral water, must strongly doubt the stories of poverty in English cricket as he enters the gates of the County Cricket Club at Edgbaston. The atmosphere reeks of wealth and prosperity and as one wanders around this monument, carefully planned by several shrewd Midland industrialists thanks to the enormous grants handed over by the supporters association, one is aware that Edgbaston is far and away the best appointed Test ground in the country. The facilities for players, members, paying public, Press, Radio and Television are second to none and there is an air of efficiency in each of the administration offices. The staggering cash flow from the highly successful Supporters Association has transformed the County Headquarters but unfortunately has been unable to purchase a County side to achieve the results the Midland supporters expect. They have, of course, had their moments with two successes in their four Gillette Cup final appearances, but have drawn a blank in the Benson & Hedges competition and most surprising of all, have never made any kind of show in the John Player League.

The Club has spared little cost and has gone overboard in its quest for overseas international Test players. If this policy was correct no one in their right mind could doubt the wisdom of their choice. Kanhai and Kallicharan, Murray and Gibbs are world class performers in any type of cricket and to add to that quartet Jameson, Amiss and Mike Smith gives the basis of a side that must surely carry most people's money in a limited-over game, where the scoring of runs at a reasonable rate is a prime factor. It has been suggested that with an array of batsmen such as this and only Lance Gibbs able seriously to turn his arm over, the team has had a lopsided look and there is no doubt that the really successful one-day sides have included a fair percentage of cricketers who could 'do a bit of both'. For all that Warwickshire can still point to David Brown and Bob Willis as two Test opening bowlers although, of course, they both reached their peak a few years apart. Willis' long absence through injury was a serious blow.

If their bowling attack has not been brilliant it has certainly been competent and one could reflect that with their heavy guns in this batting order there must be few totals that they could not chase successfully if their overall policy was to bat second in a limited-over game. My own view is that there has never been sufficient pressure on their batting stars. Amiss and Jameson, I am sure, must have taken guard on many occasions with the thought that if they should fail then one of the others was bound to make good. Thus a lapse of concentration followed by another quick wicket and before one realises what has happened Mike Smith or Derek Murray are engaged in a rearguard action with only the tailend batsmen to come. As ever it is easy to be wise after the event, but in the early seventies had Warwickshire signed Roberts in place of his colleague Kallicharan, the balance of the side would have been perfect.

With the retirement of Mike Smith and the years beginning to creep up on Rohan Kanhai, it may seem strange to consider that Warwickshire may soon be challenging again for further honours. Will the emphasis on homebred talent and a reduction in the number of overseas players pay better dividends? I am sure it will. A pace attack built around Willis, Rouse and Perryman together with the greatly improved spin bowling of

Eddie Hemmings, who has proved such a capable replacement for Lance Gibbs, will help to give the side a more balanced look. By no means the least of Warwickshire's large assets can be found in the person of one of the best cricket coaches in the world, the former Sussex all-rounder Alan Oakman. It must have been frustrating for him to scour the County in search of local talent, spend long and patient hours bringing his band of youngsters along in the knowledge that there would be few opportunities for any of them in a County side containing five English and four West Indian Test cricketers. Perhaps from now on his patience may be well rewarded.

Worcestershire

Throughout my playing career I never knew what to expect when I arrived on the New Road ground. A run of successes was quite likely to be rudely halted, and yet there were other occasions when it seemed there was no hope of a result and we returned to London with hours to spare and valuable points in the bag. Nothing has changed for me in this respect, for if assessing the prospects of any Worcestershire fixture on television, I am certain to be wrong nine times out of ten. I am sure the County will continue to baffle me for the rest of my days.

Each year I have taken a long hard look at their playing strength and each year decided that on that perfect Worcester batting pitch, they must find it difficult with a limited attack to be a successful side. Yet, quite apart from winning the County championship three times in 12 years, they have carried off the John Player League and appeared in three Lords Cup Finals. I cannot help feeling that despite this fine record their selection committee must continually harbour grave doubts about their bowling strength. In the space of four seasons and in various permutations they used no less than 15 bowlers – the equivalent of most County's entire playing staff. Brain and Holder, Cumbes and Inchmore, Carter and Pridgeon, Shutt and D'Oliveira, Hemsley and Imran, Wilkinson and Ormond and Gifford, Griffith and Johnson. To further substantiate this argument take the case of Brian Brain. He made his debut in 1959 but departed in

1960. He was signed again in 1963 yet left again in 1971. For the third time he rejoined the staff in 1973 and after bowling better than at any time in his career, he was suddenly sacked in 1975. Rodney Cass, the wicketkeeper and the useful Jim Yardley also got their marching orders much to the surprise and disgust of thousands of Worcester followers. All of which points to the fact that life as a professional bowler with Worcester is not exactly a bed of roses. Despite the ill feeling surrounding the special meetings held prior to the 1976 season, who can say that Worcester were wrong? Their reliance on new blood was fully justified with the advance of Imran Khan as one of the most successful all-rounders in the country. He bowled beautifully and put together some electrifying innings. Throughout the many comings and goings, the bowling bankers have been Vanburn Holder, Basil D'Oliveira and Norman Gifford. The first named has done remarkably well, so often picking up an early wicket and generally proving too speedy and accurate when late order batsmen have been trying to push the score along. Basil, over the years, has remained a model of consistency and it is hard to imagine his bowling ever being off target or inaccurate. Norman Gifford was quick to appreciate the impact of one-day cricket and it seems he has dovetailed his leg spin bowling to meet the requirements to the detriment of his performances in three- and five-day matches. For six years he has captained the side skilfully and, with a cheery smile for one and all, has proved a most popular skipper.

If there still remains a large question mark in my own mind about Worcestershire's bowling there is no such query about their batting. Glenn Turner is a player of the highest class and with his erstwhile partner Ron Headley saw Worcester safely away with many fine opening partnerships. The performances of Basil D'Oliveira speak for themselves, Alan Ormrod has matured with age into a highly dependable player and has more than made good Headley's departure. What a shame that soccer player Ted Hemsley has not been able to concentrate fully on the summer game. In his limited appearances over the years one has had the distinct impression that with more cricket he could have gone very close to an England cap. Headley's surprise resignation was a bitter blow to the

County and with Basil D'Oliveira approaching the twilight of his career, there seems to be a crack or two appearing in the batting order. As long as the New Road wicket remains one of the best in the land, there is every chance that some of the younger players will soon begin to make the most of it. I hope they do, otherwise it seems to me that Worcestershire may struggle to retain their fine one-day record, but having said that and remembering how often they have fooled me in the past, they may well go on to win everything in sight.

Yorkshire

When one-day cricket finally became an integral part of the English cricket season, Yorkshire for once in a while had ceased to become a power in the land. That in its simplest form is the reason why a County which has dominated first class cricket throughout this century can only look back to 1965 and 1969 for their solitary successes in the Gillette Cup. There have, of course, been many alternative and complicated theories put forward, the most surprising of all coming from their former captain, Brian Close, who asserted that they were slow to appreciate how to play limited-over cricket. The various Yorkshire Leagues, for generations the most wonderful of training grounds, have always played first of all time-limited cricket, and later limited-over cricket. To be successful in League cricket, therefore and come to the notice of the County Club the young batsman must be able to keep the scoreboard ticking over and the promising bowler able to bowl his overs accurately – vital qualifications for County one-day cricket.

For some time it has seemed to me that Yorkshire were scarcely concerned with the departure of Yorkshire-born cricketers to other Counties and in their halcyon days replacements were readily available. The real crunch for them came when they could never find amongst a mediocre bunch of Colts any player likely to replace overnight Ray Illingworth, Barry Wood, Chris Balderstone and Brian Close himself. As a result a heavy burden has fallen on the shoulders of Boycott and Hampshire and the majority of their victories have been achieved when one or the other has been on song. In the 1965

Gillette Final it was Boycott who really called the tune and his 146 at Lords must rank as the greatest ever Gillette Cup innings. If these two seniors have fought back to hold a suspect batting order together, then seamer Tony Nicholson deserves equal praise for his heroic efforts with the ball. Alert, accurate and the ability to conjure a little movement on the best of pitches there can have been few better bowlers of his type in limited-over cricket. I certainly have never seen him collared. With his departure from the scene the way is wide open for Chris Old finally to fulfil his promise with bat and ball. This most talented of cricketers is a lively and dangerous bowler but I believe yet to blossom forth as the reliable middle order batsman that his County needs.

If the last 10 years have been lean ones for Yorkshire, there are now definite signs of better things to come. Richard Lumb improves year by year, Bill Athey seems a great prospect and David Bairstow must before long catch the selectors' eyes.

Graham Stevenson looms large as an exciting young player whilst Phil Carrick should establish himself as one of the country's leading spin bowlers. If the efforts of coach Doug Padgett can unearth from the nursery a young bowler of real pace and a batsman of character then it cannot be too long before the trophy cupboard at Leeds is once again well stocked.

Future Thoughts

The most urgent requirement for our cricket authorities at the present time is a re-assessment of the structure of first class cricket in England. It must by now be patently obvious to all that one-day cricket or limited-over cricket has a vital and important role in our domestic season with a particular emphasis on the revenue it provides to the Counties.

It must also be obvious that successful as instant cricket has been, it can never be a means of producing Test match cricketers in the same way as the tried and trusted County championship programme. I am sure it is no coincidence that we have now gone through two glorious English summers without registering a solitary Test match victory. 1975 and 1976 have been boom years for cricket in every sense, with one exception. The sun has shone consistently on packed grounds and from every avenue the cash has flowed into the coffers, but unless the performance of our cricketers at top level improves considerably, interest will again begin to diminish. One cannot blame the players, who will by and large always play to the best of their ability, but rather we should look at the system which at the moment is not producing cricketers of sufficient class and quality at the very top level. If the overall standard of our game has shown an improvement over the last 20 years, few people could seriously argue the important fact that we have failed to produce the really talented performers.

The situation is not unlike the present soccer scene where we have a host of ultra-fit footballers who have mastered the basics but lack the flair and genius which takes them into the ranks of the Finneys, Bests or the Greaves of bygone years. The records of the South Americans and the Europeans surely prove that their insistence on the superior skills of the individuals rather than the enthusiastic team man will always pay better dividends at top level.

In cricket, therefore, we have to adjust our balance of fixtures to give our young players the opportunity to improve their techniques, and finally to measure up to the requirements of Test cricket. We can only succeed if we offer them the opportunity of regular competition in a type of game and under similar conditions to those of Test match cricket. The suggestion put forward by a working party of the Surrey C.C.C. to the Test and County Cricket Board comes nearer than anything I have yet seen to achieving this result.

One of their chief complaints is that, with our present system, there is insufficient County cricket prior to the first Test match and also that the introduction of the 100 overs maximum has had a detrimental effect on our own young middle order batsmen. This applies particularly when the earlier batting positions are occupied by imported overseas players. Surrey C.C.C. also believe that a County championship programme covering 20 three-day games is illogical and unsatisfactory. The suggestion is that the present three-day County Championship should be replaced by a four-day championship of 16 games with each County playing the others. This would allow these matches to be played under conditions nearer to a five-day Test Match. In turn this would improve the standard of our Test team, give greater opportunities to spin bowlers and place a greater emphasis on winning matches by bowling sides out. The last two points have been more than lost by the introduction of one-day cricket.

The above are just a few of many proposals put forward by a working party under the chairmanship of Raman Subba Row and are the ones I am in agreement with. To show in further detail how a County programme would look in the future, I have set out here a fixture list for a County based on the last cricket season when the West Indians were the tourists.

Allocation has been made for 20 four-day first class fixtures all commencing on a Friday. Of these, 16 matches would be played within the framework of the County Championship, and two more would be taken up by those counties on the tourists' fixture list and for the counties fixture against one of the Universities. This would leave two completely free weeks for any juggling of fixtures which may be necessary. Players would thus be playing up to six four-day matches prior to the first Test match and with County matches due to start on a Friday, Test match players would only be missing from their County sides for a maximum of five matches.

To ensure that members were getting value for their subscriptions the large percentage of home games would be played at the County's principal home ground where there is obviously a better chance of preparing a good wicket capable of lasting for four days. One-day fixtures could then be played on one of the minor, or country grounds. The basic one-day fixtures remain unaltered with 19 Sundays allocated for the 16 John Player matches. Benson & Hedges Cup cricket would again extend over the first 10 weeks of the season and Gillette Cup cricket would cover the second half of the season.

There is, of course, no way in which one could introduce a new 100 per cent foolproof format for our summer game and there is no doubt that the above scheme will have its critics. It is offered as a means of helping to improve the standard of our cricket and also to help redress the balance of our game which, in recent years, has leaned a little too heavily in favour of our one-day cricket. From the conversations I have had with our players it is a move which would be welcomed by the large majority.

Date	T	C	Event
April			
23		C[1]	
24		C	
25			
26		C	
27		C	
28			B/H(Z)
29			
30		C[2]	
May			
1		C	
2			JP
3		C	
4		C	
5			B/H(Z)
6			
7		C[3]	
8		C	
9			JP
10		C	
11		C	
12			B/H(Z)
13			
14		C[4]	
15		C	
16			JP
17		C	
18		C	
19			B/H(Z)
20			
21		C[5]	
22		C	
23			JP
24		C	
25		C	
26			B/H(Z)
27			
28		C[6]	
29		C	
30			JP
31		C	
June			
1		C	
2			
3	T		
4	T	C[7]	
5	T	C	
6			JP
7	T	C	
8	T	C	
9			B/H($\frac{1}{4}$)
10			
11		C[8]	
12		C	
13			JP
14		C	
15		C	
16	T		
17	T		
18	T	C[9]	
19	T	C	
20			JP
21	T	C	
22	T	C	
23			B/H(s/f)
24			
25		C[10]	
26		C	
27			JP
28		C	
29		C	
30			
July			
1			
2		C[11]	
3		C	
4			JP
5		C	
6		C	
7			
8	T		
9	T	C[12]	
10	T	C	
11			JP
12	T	C	
13	T	C	
14			G/C
15			
16		C[13]	
17		C	B/H(F)
18			JP
19		C	
20		C	
21			
22	T		
23	T	C[14]	
24	T	C	
25			JP
26	T	C	
27	T	C	
28			G/C
29			
30		C[15]	
31		C	
August			
1			JP
2		C	
3		C	
4			G/C
5			
6		C[16]	
7		C	
8			JP
9		C	
10		C	
11			
12	T		
13	T	C[17]	
14	T	C	
15			JP
16	T	C	
17	T	C	
18			
19			
20		C[18]	
21		C	
22			JP
23		C	
24		C	
25			G/C(s/f)
26			
27		C[19]	
28		C	
29			JP
30		C	
31		C	

September

1
2
3 C^{20}
4 C   G/C(F)
5   JP
6 C
7 C
8
9
10

T = Test Matches
C = 4-day County
     matches
B/H(Z) = Benson &
          Hedges
          Cup
          (Zonal)
G/C = Gillette Cup
JP = John Player
     League

Index